CHASING GREATNESS

Karch Kiraly
with Don Patterson

VOLLEYBALL

THEARTOFCOACHINGVOLLEYBALL.COM

Printed in the United States of America

First Printing, December 2022

ISBN: 978-1-7347652-5-0

Written by Karch Kiraly with Don Patterson

Published by Total Sports, LLC
330 Encinitas Boulevard, Suite 102
Encinitas, CA 92024

www.theartofcoachingvolleyball.com

Cover photo credit: FIVB

To Janna, my wife and favorite person ever, and our sons Kristian and Kory. You three opened up a whole new world of learning for me – the coaching world. Thank you!
–Karch Kiraly

To my wife, Kendal, our daughter, Alex, and son, Andrew, who inspire me to keep trying my hardest.
–Don Patterson

CONTENTS

1 Introduction

5 Chapter 1: Learning It, Earning It

11 Chapter 2: Making Every Minute Count

19 Chapter 3: Practicing Purposefully

29 Chapter 4: Embracing Adversity

47 Chapter 5: Developing Willpower

59 Chapter 6: Learning from Mistakes

69 Chapter 7: Playing to Strengths, Overcoming Weaknesses

81 Chapter 8: Carrying Yourself with Confidence

89 Chapter 9: Managing Less Productive Thoughts

99 Chapter 10: Being a Good Teammate

113 Chapter 11: Preparing to Be Your Best

139 Chapter 12: Organizing for Success

155 Chapter 13: Learning by Doing

165 Chapter 14: Inspiration

173 Chapter 15: Go for It!

INTRODUCTION

It would be understandable if some pointed questions immediately come to mind as you encounter this book. One: Why would I write about greatness? My answer would be, because I've spent so much of my life pursuing mastery and human flourishing. While the pursuit never ends, and regularly falls short, it's immensely rewarding. That pursuit is what keeps me going.

Pursuing "better" and refusing to be satisfied with "maintaining" my current level are key elements in leading a successful and fulfilling life. As economist and social commentator Thomas Sowell has pointed out, prehistoric people had the exact same natural resources available that humanity has now but had almost none of the things we take for granted – like the ability to feed and clothe eight billion people, electricity, and intercontinental travel and communication. The pursuit of better – through hard work, learning, creativity, setbacks, persistence – led us to where we are today.

Something else that adds substance to the "why write a book" answer is that volleyball is a team sport. Almost everything we do in life is with other people, with teammates. Our families are teams. Our circles of friends are teams. Our classrooms are teams of teachers and students. We form teams at work – etc., etc., etc. Understanding that we're social creatures, that we need to be in groups to survive, and that we can't do it alone because we're far stronger together, adds even more weight to my answer. Having been immersed in volleyball for well over five decades, the pursuit of team excellence – team greatness, if you will – has always been my overriding focus.

Kiraly family photo

My wife Janna, my teammate for life. Great teammates make people around them way better, with support, with challenge, and with honest counsel and feedback. Nobody does that better. I'm a lucky guy.

Another question that could easily come to mind: What's with the word "greatness" in the title? I don't think of myself as great. Instead, I try to convey a sense of humility through actions and words. I'm reminded of this quote by psychologist Adam Grant: "Go in being humble. I may be wrong." Regardless, I can live with that word, based on this caveat: I am not by any stretch claiming to have all the answers on greatness, on mastery, on flourishing, but, with an assist from my co-author, Don Patterson, I *will* share strategies that have helped me be better over the course of a long career, strategies I hope can be applied and modified to help others, others like you the reader.

So with that, let's dive in!

CHAPTER 1
LEARNING IT, EARNING IT

Let's begin with this obvious fact: Babies don't know how to crawl when they're born. In fact, newborn babies have only the most basic reflexes and instincts. When you consider the path they take to master rudimentary life skills, it becomes clear that despite their apparent helplessness, they are relentless learning machines.

Think about how babies *do* learn to crawl. It takes great effort. They work their little rear ends off and fail and fail and fail, until they finally get it. There are no shortcuts. They don't let setbacks or frustration shut them down. They just keep trying.

Once babies have conquered crawling, the next frontier is walking, so they plunge in and follow the same process: try, fail, try, fail, try, fail – and, finally, succeed. They can't get frustrated with each setback. They *don't* get frustrated with each setback. They just keep trying.

This process was so long ago for most of us that maybe it demands a reminder: *You and I* were those babies, learning to crawl and walk, failing, and relentlessly trying.

What's the point? It's that mastery is often misunderstood. It's far less about genetics than many people might think. It's mostly about hard work and persistence.

Another example comes from the archives of baseball legend Joe DiMaggio, who played for the New York Yankees from 1936 to 1951. "Joltin' Joe," as he is known by old-time baseball fans, still holds the major league record for consecutive games with a hit: 56. Baseball historians consider him to be one of the greatest players of all time. When a reporter once asked DiMaggio about being a "natural hitter," he promptly took the reporter to his dimly lit basement, grabbed a bat and began taking swings. Before each swing, he would call out the imaginary pitch – "slider, inside" or "fastball, high and away." With each call, he made slight adjustments to his grip and stance before swinging. When he was finished, he made a tally mark on the wall next to thousands of others he'd made in previous sessions, then turned to the reporter and said, "Don't ever call me a natural hitter again."

In telling this story, I don't mean to imply that hard work is everything and genetics is no factor. What you get biologically from your parents absolutely affects the limits of your abilities. For example, if you happen to be 6-foot-2, you're probably never going to be one of the world's top gymnasts. You might become a very good gymnast, but not one of the best, because 6-2 is too tall to perfect many of the moves needed to reach world class level. But you can certainly improve the moves in your repertoire, and add new ones.

Similarly, if you're 5-4, you're probably not going to be a star in the NBA or WNBA.

The message I want to get across is that EVERYBODY, regardless of their genetic makeup, is capable of making massive improvements in any skill. To do that most effectively, I believe the process demands the following:

1. Deploy a purposeful learning strategy. (More on that later.)
2. Apply consistent, focused effort toward specific changes.
3. Invest a significant amount of time.

Number 3 warrants some elaboration. When I say "significant" time, I mean a LOT. It's universally understood by those who have studied the subject of mastery that it takes thousands and thousands of hours to become a master in whatever endeavor you're pursuing, whether it's sports, music, chess, brain surgery or anything else.

Given this extraordinary commitment of time and energy, I have always admired athletes who are able to sustain excellence and stay at an elite level for long periods of time. Three stand out to me:

Tom Brady – The New England Patriots selected Brady in the sixth round of the 2000 NFL Draft with the 199th pick. That means there were 198 players chosen ahead of him, including six other quarterbacks who have long since retired from the game. In 21 seasons through 2021, Brady won more Super Bowls (seven) and played in more Super Bowls (10) than any other quarterback in NFL history. His most recent championship came February 7, 2021, when, at age 43, he led the Tampa

Bay Buccaneers to an upset of the defending-champion Kansas City Chiefs. One story I've heard about Brady goes all the way back to his rookie season with the Patriots. Between and after practices at training camp, coaches noticed that the young quarterback was directing extra training sessions with other non-starters so they could work on skills, master the offensive playbook and be better prepared to compete for starting positions. That kind of dedication – taking the initiative to go above and beyond what's requested of you – helped Brady become a quarterback who most consider the greatest ever.

LeBron James – In nearly two decades in the NBA through 2022, James won four championships with three different franchises (Miami, Cleveland and Los Angeles) and has been considered the best player in basketball for more than a decade. I saw an article recently comparing playoff statistics of the top NBA players in the 21st century. LeBron was first in points, assists, defensive rebounds and steals and second in 3-pointers. This shows consistent and diverse excellence over time, and it also indicates how well he prepares and conditions his body to maintain that standard. I watched an interesting YouTube video a while back in which he was working with retired NBA great Hakeem Olajuwon on post moves. My understanding is that it's common for LeBron to devote time in the offseason to adding new parts to his already wide and deep skill set. Keep in mind, his seasons have almost always been among the longest in the league because his teams usually progress deep into the playoffs, reach the finals or win the championship. So he needs to be that much more durable because he is playing longer than most other players. At 38, he remains an incredibly elite performer, and his dedication to health, fitness and improvement has played a big role in his career longevity.

Kerri Walsh Jennings – In our sport of volleyball, no one has set a higher standard of sustained excellence than Kerri. She competed in five Olympics, one with the U.S. indoor team at the 2000 Games in Sydney, and four on the beach, where she won three gold medals (with Misty May-Treanor in 2004, 2008, 2012) and a bronze (with April Ross in 2016). Kerri's story is obviously one of longevity, but one of my favorite moments of her career came at the Rio Olympics in 2016 when she and April suffered a soul-crushing semifinal loss to Brazil's Agatha Bednarczuk and Barbara Seixas De Freitas. It was Kerri's first Olympic beach loss ever, but she found a way to bounce back less than 24 hours later to defeat another top Brazilian team: Talita Antunes and Larissa Franca. In 2021, Kerri fell just one place short of qualifying for a sixth Olympics, in Tokyo.

DEFINING GREATNESS

Now that you've read about some elite athletes who have reached the pinnacle, I should clarify that I don't view greatness as synonymous with being one of the best ever. Greatness is both relative and absolute. If you're striving for relative greatness, you may not need to even be the best in your own household to achieve greatness in a chosen skill. You simply have to continually work toward reaching your potential and accomplishing your goals.

Here's an example: Let's say an 18-year-old college freshman decides she wants to learn French, studies it for four years, maybe even spends time studying in France for greater immersion. After that amount of time and intense study, the student will likely have achieved relative greatness if you compare her level of French speaking to the zero level that she had before she started studying.

At the same time, in absolute terms, would a student like that be so proficient that she could work at the United Nations as a simultaneous translator and instantly convert French to her native English? Probably not. Having started at age 18 and trained just four years in college doesn't yet get you to that level of absolute greatness.

This distinction between absolute and relative greatness is an important one. Absolute greatness implies world-class, Olympic-medal levels of skill, something few people actually achieve. On the other hand, relative greatness is within anyone's reach in countless pursuits: parenting, foreign languages, sports, musical instruments – the list is endless.

If you've set a goal to be as good as you can be at something within the parameters of internal factors – like genetics – and external factors – like the amount of time you've put in – you can take great pride in the improvements you've made and the levels you've reached. Every time you add a new skill or improve an existing one, you earn more confidence, enhance your learning abilities and increase your chances for success. That's true in sports, school, your job or anything you might want to get good at in everyday life.

It's the same process that worked for all of us when we were babies learning to crawl, and it keeps on working as long as we keep working at learning.

CHAPTER 2

MAKING EVERY MINUTE COUNT

My very last practice with the USA men's national team was sub-par. That, at least, was the opinion of our head coach, Bill Neville, who chewed us all out on that day in 1989 for what he felt was a lack of focus and lackluster play.

I had already announced my retirement from the national team and was finishing the final training block before beginning a new chapter of my career, which brought me back to the beach game, where I competed professionally until 2007, and took me to Italy for two seasons of indoor volleyball as a member of one of the world's top club teams, Il Messaggero Ravenna.

It wasn't typical for our USA team to just go through the motions in practice. Our trademark – and a source of great pride for us throughout the 1980s – was bringing an astronomical level of intensity to the gym every day, without fail. In fact, we were so intense that it occasionally reached a boiling point. There were times when we screamed at each other non-stop during drills and scrimmages, and that led to some collateral damage. For example, during one fiery three-week pre-Olympic training camp in 1984, we dished out so much verbal abuse to the ref, Gary Colberg, that we all felt it necessary at the end of camp to write our apologies on a volleyball, even though it lacked the necessary surface area for adequate remorse. This isn't an atmosphere I would encourage today. Times have changed. But it clearly worked for us back then. We cultivated extreme urgency for improvement by pushing each other to the limit, which was imperative in our quest to become the best team on the planet.

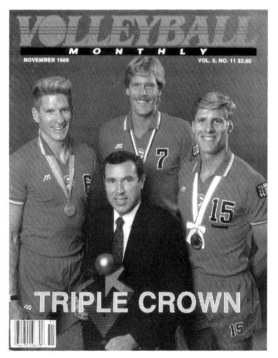

Our dominant U.S. team in the 1980s (clockwise from left, Steve Timmons, Craig Buck, me and coach Marv Dunphy) brought maximum intensity to every minute of every practice.

And we did just that, dominating international volleyball for a good part of the decade with gold medals at the 1984 and 1988 Olympics, the 1985 World Cup and the 1986 World Championship.

Given that hyper-competitive atmosphere that we had all thrived on, it stung to hear Bill say we had come up short in my final practice. In fact, it bothered me so much that I called him that night to get a more detailed explanation. His first words were: "Karch, that was your *last* practice. Why are you even calling me? I only chewed on you because I had already gotten on everybody else." My response, as Bill remembers it, was, "Because I'm always looking to get better."

That was my mindset then, and I still strive for that mindset today. It was instilled in me early in my career by our coach at Santa Barbara High School, Rick Olmstead, who placed great importance on outworking the competition and making every minute count. It certainly never would have occurred to me to decrease my effort based on circumstances – in this case, the fact that it was my final USA practice.

To this day, I regularly seek information and feedback from coaches, teammates, players I'm coaching, mentors and outside sources. At the end of some one-on-one meetings with an athlete or assistant coach, I ask for feedback by saying: "How can I be better for you?" Other questions I might ask are:

- "What do you need to be coached on next?"
- "What's something you really like that I do or say for you?"
- "What's something you really *don't* like that I do or say?"

Our staff has found it useful to give players anonymous polls and surveys. This helps them feel comfortable being completely candid when it comes to assessing our coaching methods. We would never hold it against a player for offering an honest critique, but you can see where athletes, especially those who might be new to the program, would be reluctant to criticize coaches who will ultimately decide their standing on the team.

For me, the bottom line is simple: Feedback of any kind is valuable. The more I can get, the more I believe I'll be able to adjust my preparation and get better at my job.

NO END IN SIGHT

I also find it helpful to keep in mind that you're never going to cross a finish line while pursuing greatness. That's both the fun and the frustration of it. It's an infinite project – like a martial art, where even becoming a black belt isn't a final destination. Next is second-degree, then third-degree and so on.

Thinking of greatness as a never-ending pursuit provides a built-in motivation that doesn't hinge on firing up for an individual match or tournament or award. It goes deeper, allowing your motivational foundation to be formulated on a desire to get better every day rather than on a string of rewards that may or may not happen.

I'm not saying that winning matches and trophies shouldn't be on your list of goals, nor am I saying that they shouldn't be sources of motivation. I'm just pointing out that sustained enthusiasm for mastering a craft involves a significant amount of intrinsic motivation, which is about doing something for the enjoyment of learning and getting better. That kind of motivation, in my view, is more sustainable.

A fire of motivation can be lit when you see someone else do something well and think, "I'd like to do that too." This in itself is a nice lesson. If you can enjoy the accomplishments of others in a way that motivates you rather than becoming jealous that they're doing something that you can't, it helps you frame the process around learning. Instead of comparing, you can focus on what's important to your development – "How much better can I make this skill?"

In the USA women's national team gym, one of our preferred learning strategies is focused tutoring sessions. These target specific skills that we think are critically important to success in volleyball. For instance, first-touches that set the tone for every rally: serving, passing and digging. Often, our tutoring sessions focus on just one detail of a technical skill. We also like to keep them short, about 10-15 minutes. Research tells us that learning is more productive in small chunks rather than in long, repetitive sessions that challenge our ability to stay on task.

Tied in with our tutoring sessions are training periods modeled after a learning process you might find in school. We name them accordingly: "Attack School," "Defensive School," etc. In these sessions, we urge players to experiment and explore new things – skills or details of skills that aren't necessarily strengths and, therefore, aren't "comfortable." We want to send a message to everyone that it's OK to make mistakes. It's our belief that if you're not messing up sometimes, it's too easy and comfortable, and you're not working at the edge of your abilities.

This mindset, of course, is applicable to any type of learning. Many of our national team players compete overseas on professional club teams in countries like Italy, Turkey, China, Japan and Brazil. To better enjoy the experience, some of them put great effort toward learning the local language. This requires a fearlessness that doesn't dwell on the potential embarrassment of making mistakes. To become more fluent in the language, they have to speak it. When they speak it, they'll make mistakes. Knowing what mistakes they've made is a huge learning accelerator. How do they know their mistakes? An effective strategy is to ask their teammates for feedback. The point is, as learners, they're not paralyzed by fear of failure. They dive in, get muddy, screw it up. And by failing faster, they get better faster.

A CHALLENGE ON TOP OF A CHALLENGE

Competing in sports has an additional challenge beyond just the pursuit of greatness. When the teams are evenly matched, the outcome will be uncertain, so there's always the possibility that your team will lose. Losing not only doesn't feel good, it often can just plain hurt. So if you're too wrapped up in the results, the discouragement of losses can disrupt the larger goal of training and preparing to get better. For that matter, so can wins. Basking in the glory of victory can be equally problematic, especially if it leads to an overconfidence that prevents you from working as hard as you should to keep improving.

The fact is, wins and losses might not tell us that much about our progress. We could win but play lousy and display no improvement in areas we've been working on, or we could even have regressed. Conversely, we could lose and play quite well and/or display significant improvement. Concentrating on the process of improvement rather than wins and losses allows us to stay focused on what's most important: getting a little better every day.

Another way to look at it is that we can't completely control the results, but we can influence them. It doesn't do us much good to stew over a loss or a losing streak. What matters is continuing to trust the process and working on getting better at the specific things that will eventually help change the results.

If you're looking for inspiration as to what's possible in the area of dramatic improvement, take it from the 2001 New England Patriots. In 2000, they finished dead last in the AFC East division of the NFL with a record of 5-11. One year later, with the addition of rookie quarterback Tom Brady and a second-year head coach, Bill Belichick, the Patriots won the division with an 11-5 record, then went 3-0 in the playoffs to win the Super Bowl. It was the first title in franchise history and the beginning of a dynasty that has now won six NFL championships.

A lot of factors played a role in the Patriots' success, but one of the big keys to the turnaround was that Belichick changed the culture to more of a meritocracy that favored earning your spot through hard work as opposed to owning your spot on the basis of past results and seniority. The philosophy shift was described this way in "The Education of a Coach" by David Halberstam:

"Belichick had been appalled at the beginning of (his) first season in New England by how many players could not finish

their conditioning drills – say 20 sprints of 40 yards, done with a certain time limit – and had simply collapsed on the field and did not even try to get up and finish them; worse, they did not think it was that important. There had been an attitude among all too many players, (Belichick) had decided, that 'I'm a starter, I own my job and you can't bench me or even rotate me.'"

This highlights a key point when it comes to embracing a growth mindset: Your job, no matter what you're trying to become great in, is to show up and do whatever it takes to improve. Don't focus on yesterday, last week or last year. Don't expect success based on past successes. Don't expect failure based on past failures. Just prepare, work hard each and every minute, and strive to become an ever-better version of yourself.

CHAPTER 3

PRACTICING PURPOSEFULLY

No doubt you've heard the saying, "Practice makes perfect." I'd say that's a bit misleading. More accurate would be "Practice makes permanent." Research tells us that the key to mastery is not just about logging large blocks of time practicing – it's about doing the *right* kind of practice.

An expert on this subject was Anders Ericsson, a cognitive psychologist who did extensive research on learning methodology and co-authored "Peak: Secrets from the New Science of Expertise," a book I highly recommend. His work was the foundation for Malcolm Gladwell's bestseller "Outliers: The Story of Success," which popularized the notion that it takes 10,000 hours to achieve mastery. Many who read "Outliers" took away an overly simplistic understanding of Ericsson's work. Ericsson didn't conclude that simply logging many thousands of hours is the ticket to mastery. He concluded that people can become masters if they invest that amount of time toward *deliberate* or *purposeful* practice. That's an important distinction.

Before we dive deeper into the how-tos of deliberate or purposeful learning, let's define our terms. To Ericsson, the word "deliberate" was reserved for fields that have been studied for a very long time and have developed proven methods of achieving mastery. Playing the piano would be a good example. Because of the vast amount of musical study that has been done in the decades and centuries since the likes of Mozart, Beethoven and Bach composed their timeless works, the blueprint for learning to play classical music is extremely refined. With volleyball, it's different. Yes, the sport is more than a hundred years old, but teaching methods applied to the game have only been formally studied for the last several decades – not nearly enough time to produce a definitive curriculum. With that in mind, I use the same word Ericsson did, "purposeful" instead of "deliberate," when referring to volleyball. The concepts are applied in the same way, but the methodology is still a work in progress.

To streamline my thoughts on purposeful learning, I've organized them in 7 steps:

STEP 1: LEARN FROM THE GREATS

A good starting point for establishing purposeful practice habits is to study the masters. If you're focusing on passing in volleyball, for instance, task number one is to identify some world-class passers. From my era, that might be Aldis Berzins, who was the other primary serve-receiver with me on our Olympic gold medal team in 1984, or Sinjin Smith, one of the all-time great beach players. From a more current era, maybe it's Justine Wong-Orantes, the U.S.'s libero on the 2021 Olympic gold medal team. Jordan Larson would be another. She was a starting outside hitter on that same gold-medal winning team, and she also started on our bronze (2016) and silver (2012) winning Olympic teams.

Once you've found your skill models, go to YouTube, pull up some video and take a few notes. I regularly assign this task to new/younger players: Watch someone great, then ask yourself, "What can I learn from this?" Or "What's here that can make me better?"

If you're looking at passers in volleyball, you might note how the great ones always face where the ball is coming *from* rather than facing the *target*. Or how they angle their platform to reflect the ball where they want it to go. Or how they move, shuffling rather than crossing over. Look for anything that may set them apart from ordinary passers.

STEP 2: MAKE A CHECKLIST

From here, you can make a checklist of each item and create practice activities. In the national team gym, we write practice plans on a whiteboard with a little rectangular box that says "F" for "Focus" followed by a short description of the desired outcome. For example: "**F: Name, plus action**" would be a helpful focus for 3 vs. 3 over-the-net deep-court pepper. Players have to call out both the name of the next person who will touch the ball and the action wanted. The passer might say: "Justine, set!" Then Justine would say: "Jordan, hit!" This eliminates confusion and allows everybody to identify and prepare for their next task more quickly. Every time a team completes a pass-set-hit to the other side, the players rotate, so they are forced to continually think about which team-mate is where, whose name to call, and how to adjust.

STEP 3: STICK TO ONE TASK

An important point I've learned from research and experi-ence is that learning is most productive when you concen-trate on a singular purpose. It's easy for coaches to overwhelm athletes with unfocused feedback. You watch a player receive some serves, and with each pass, you notice something that could use a slight adjustment, so you offer feedback, then offer feedback on a *different* technical improvement on the next rep, and so on. Next thing you know, the player is trying to get better at five different things at once and, as a result, is getting better at nothing, probably even getting worse! As a coach, or even as a teammate who is trying to help another teammate, it's important to discipline yourself to apply laser focus to a single task.

Now, you might be thinking, "I can tackle more because I'm good at multitasking." But maybe your tasking is not as multi as you think. Sports psychologist Mike Gervais, who has worked extensively with our U.S. women's national volley-ball team as well as the Seattle Seahawks in the NFL and other top-level pro athletes, says that we humans are capable of only holding one thought in our brains at a time. In his view, when people think they're multi-tasking, they're really just sharing their focus by fractions of a second, giving a quick thought to one thing, then another, then another. Splintered thoughts crammed into short periods of time are obviously not ideal for learning.

Depending on how a player likes to learn, there are adjustments that may need to be made to training sessions. For some athletes, it's highly efficient and productive to work on one specific task until they achieve some durable change and check it off. For others, a boredom factor from too much repetition might impede progress if they're using this method. Those athletes may benefit from variety, so training might mean working on X today, Y tomorrow and Z the next day, then repeating the cycle as often as it takes to get the job done.

STEP 4: KEEP IT SHORT AND ON POINT

I've found that learning gets a boost if it is done in short spurts. After five to 10 minutes, it's good to move on to the next item on the practice list. Activities that go on too long can become monotonous and make it difficult to maintain focus, especially those that don't look like volleyball, with a serve, pass, set, hit and play on. That's when focus can fade.

As we all know, time is valuable, so it's important to use every minute wisely, no matter what you're working on. I've visited a lot of practices where teams spend the first 10 minutes jogging around the gym, then sit on the floor stretching. In my mind, these PE-like activities are mostly a waste of time because studies have shown they do very little to actually prepare – we use the word "activate" – our bodies for dynamic volleyball. And jogging and floor stretching do nothing to improve volleyball skills. Most teams don't have unlimited training time and need to use every minute efficiently – for them, why not play some short court? There are a zillion variations: 1v1, 2v2, standing, jumping; they all get people moving and give them chances to react with a good contact that keeps the ball nearby, which means their ball control is improving. That could earn the team an extra point or two in a match, and those points might be the difference between winning and losing. Remember, it's not just 10 minutes; it's 10 minutes times however many practices you have over the course of the season. If it's 50 practices, then you have added more than eight extra hours of training. That's sure to be beneficial come playoff time.

STEP 5: WORK WITH A PARTNER

Another key to purposeful practice is using a buddy system so your players are working in micro teams of two or three. This gives them a chance to get real-time feedback and encouragement – especially since there are almost always far more players than coaches, so coaches only see a small fraction of each player's actions. If one of the partners loses focus, another can get them back on task. If a technique adjustment is needed, a partner can gently guide her buddy back by asking, "What was your focus again?" If a player does something really well, there's someone there to reinforce it and say: "You nailed it! Just what you were working on." This can give them extra motivation to keep at it, especially since that feedback came from a peer.

STEP 6: FOCUS ON THE PROCESS, NOT THE OUTCOME

When you're learning, the result is not what's most important. Keep your eye on the steps you're taking to get better. For example, when working on passing, don't concern yourself with whether the ball goes to your target. Focusing too much on the result and too little on the performance – or on the process – can slow the learning procedure. Stay locked in on the process of doing one specific action, like facing where the ball is coming from or angling your platform to where you want the ball to go.

STEP 7: ASSESS YOUR PROGRESS AS YOU PRACTICE

As you practice skills, be sure to engage in self-evaluation. Keep it simple. Thumb up if you executed your focus during the task. Thumb sideways for so-so. Thumb down for sub-standard execution. Aim for a thumb up on a certain number of reps. Maybe three and a half or four out of each five. This helps keep you motivated and focused.

A resource that I've found very helpful in shaping a purposeful practice philosophy is an academic paper on golf titled "PaR (Plan-act-Review) Golf: Motor Learning Research and Improving Golf Skills." It was written by Timothy D. Lee, a professor of kinesiology at McMaster University in Canada, and Richard A. Schmidt, who was a professor and research scientist in the fields of physical education, psychology and kinesiology before his death in 2015. The major theme of the article is that practice for golf or anything else should simulate the reality, variation, and challenges of actual play, not just the rote repetition that is often carried out on the driving range, where golfers may just hit the same exact shot with the same club over and over.

The article suggests that golfers follow this three-step process:

1. **Plan** – Decide how you will execute each action.
2. **Act** – Execute the action.
3. **Review** – Review the action to determine what you did well and what needs work.

If you think about this, it makes perfect sense. A golfer – or a volleyball player – who hits the same shot again and again is on mental autopilot. That may result in a string of good shots, but it doesn't require you to see, respond and decide like you would in an actual golf tournament or volleyball match. So how much good is it doing you? Very little, in the opinion of Lee and Schmidt, who conclude that variety – for instance, hitting with a driver, then a seven iron, then chipping – will produce much greater improvement and learning. A key point they emphasize, however, is that it's not the "randomness" of the skill sequence that is achieving better results; it's the fact that the randomness "encourages the learner to plan the movement in the interval just before the practice attempt." With each new task, the authors note, you are forced to come up with a new plan rather than just re-using the previous plan. This planning is critical to learning, so the more you practice it, the more you'll benefit.

In our USA gym, we fight against autopilot mode and foster randomness in many ways. If we're working on passing, we might serve a player two balls from Zone 1, then two from Zone 6 and then two from Zone 5. Some will be short, some deep. We might vary the spin. Then we'll add other factors – like moving the target so passers have to adjust their passing angle. We might have a target in Zone 1 to simulate an extreme angle. We might place different color disks on the floor as targets and have the passer call out a new color each time. Or I might call out a color *after* the server hits the ball so the passer has to adjust quickly, both mentally and physically.

The third step in the PaR sequence, Review, gives coaches and athletes an opportunity to gather for a meaningful debriefing session that extends beyond just thumbs up, thumbs down. How did we do in this activity? What could we tweak next time to make it even more productive? Lingering questions or concerns can be covered in just a few minutes; answering them, and incorporating those answers in future sessions, will make those sessions that much more productive.

CHECK YOUR EGO AT THE DOOR

Opening yourself up to feedback isn't always comfortable. Few people who are feeling good about something they are doing enjoy hearing that they should do it differently, especially if they've already worked hard at it. But it's well worth accepting criticism from others because it provides you with a fresh perspective that will help you get better in the long run. This point is illustrated nicely by surgeon Atul Gawande in his best-selling book "The Checklist Manifesto." Five years after becoming a surgeon, he felt he was stuck and stagnanting, so he asked one of his former medical school professors to observe him during a surgery. The professor watched and took copious notes, leaving Gawande to wonder what he was doing to warrant such scrutiny. One observation was that he was holding his elbow really high, putting more strain on his arm and shoulder muscles. The former professor explained that this would make the surgeon more fatigued after several hours of surgery, and that could cause some loss of motor control. Keep in mind, Gawande was already a well-established and highly respected surgeon at this point. But he shelved his ego in the interests of getting even better. Had he not, he might have been risking more mistakes and poorer outcomes, working with greater fatigue than necessary for the next 20 years.

Along the same lines, in my experience, people who are easily embarrassed can struggle to be great learners. No surprise. If you're overly self-conscious about every mistake, whether it's mispronouncing a word in a new language or taking a wrong step on the volleyball court, you're less likely to have the resolve you'll need to keep at it until you improve. There's a good lesson there. Don't be so worried about the way you might look to others that you back down from new challenges. In the long run, your life will be far richer if you tackle the tough stuff head on.

Talking about all the different layers to productive learning reminds me of something I have heard for many years from Marv Dunphy, who was head coach of our 1988 Olympic gold medal team and a Hall of Fame collegiate coach at Pepperdine. He would say: "Volleyball players are happiest when they feel like they're improving. If you're focusing better, practicing better, getting a better return on your investment, you're going to get more joy out of it because you're going to feel yourself improving."

Words to live by – for volleyball players and everyone else.

CHAPTER 4

EMBRACING ADVERSITY

The day I decided to retire from playing beach volleyball was 10 years before I actually *did* retire. I was sitting on a bench in Wisconsin, overlooking Lake Michigan. It was July of 1997, one year after Kent Steffes and I had won the gold medal at the 1996 Atlanta Olympics. On this day, I had finished a dismal 9th at an AVP beach tournament in Milwaukee with Adam Johnson, who had become my beach partner at the beginning of that season. Like me, Adam was used to winning, and we were beaten by a team in the Milwaukee tournament that we wouldn't have lost to if I'd been playing well.

To give you the backstory, I had returned to the beach that summer after offseason shoulder surgery. This was the first shoulder surgery of my career, and astoundingly, my first volleyball-related surgery, period. I had played my first beach tournament alongside my dad at the age of 11 in 1972, and over the next 25 years, I took hundreds of thousands of swings, competing at the highest levels of both indoor and beach volleyball. My shoulder had held up valiantly but finally surrendered at the end of the 1996 season, just three weeks after Kent and I won the gold in Atlanta. Post-surgery, I had a long offseason of physical therapy and rehab, then began training for the 1997 season. In my absence, Kent played with Brazilian star Jose Loiola, a very gifted player who was once described by beach pro Canyon Ceman as "athletically superior to the entire world." Jose was the guy who could jump up – from the soft sand – and cup his hand over the top of the net antenna. If you don't think that takes some serious hops, try it sometime! Jose and Kent were having great success together, so I didn't hold it against Kent when he told me he was going to stick with Jose.

When Adam and I began playing together in 1997, I could tell something was different in my offense. Before the shoulder surgery, when I took a swing, I knew within a foot or two where the ball would land. My shoulder had always been unusually loose; among other repairs, the surgery tightened up the architecture in the joint. That restricted my range of motion and prevented me from reaching as high, which meant I would take swings and watch the ball go pretty much anywhere but where I wanted it to go – five feet farther to the left or right, or maybe several feet longer or shorter. It was extremely frustrating, and I felt horrible that I was letting Adam down and ruining our team's chances.

When we got eliminated from the Milwaukee tournament, I could have paid a $250 change fee to switch to an earlier flight home, but I felt it was a waste of money in light of how little I had made for the family during that tournament – less than $2,000, not a big paycheck when you factor in travel expenses, hotel, meals, etc. To kill some time, I drove around until I spotted that bench on a bluff overlooking Lake Michigan. I sat there for what was probably three or four hours and had a meeting with myself. I made peace with the fact that I was never again going to come close to playing at the level I'd played at for so many years, so I decided it was time to retire. I'd had an amazing run. At 36, I'd played far longer than I ever thought I would.

I flew home and talked about it with my wife, Janna. We discussed my exit plan. I would finish the season, then announce my retirement. I wasn't looking to have a "Farewell to Karch" tour with ceremonies and speeches. I just wanted to compete as well as I could for the remaining tournaments and then look ahead to the next chapter, whatever that might be.

The very next weekend, the AVP tournament was in Hermosa Beach, California, just an hour up the road from our home in San Clemente. Guess what? Adam and I won. Not bad for a guy who thought he was washed up a week earlier! The next weekend, the AVP Tour stop was in Sacramento. We won there, too. A week after that we were in Vail, Colorado. Again, we won. One week later, we won again, this time in Minneapolis. Four weeks, four wins.

Not only were we winning, we were beating very good teams. In two of the finals, we defeated Kent and Jose, the dominant team on tour. In another, we beat Dain Blanton and Eric Fonoimoana, who won an Olympic gold medal together three years later in Sydney, Australia. And the win in Hermosa Beach came against future Olympic gold medalist Todd Rogers and his original partner, Dax Holdren, who also went on to represent the U.S. in the Olympics.

It won't surprise you to hear that I reevaluated my retirement plans after that four-week stretch. And the lesson I want to emphasize here is that patience in the face of adversity is an essential attribute for anyone aspiring to mastery. In all the tournaments through the Milwaukee event, I had been putting tremendous pressure on myself, trying as hard as I could to reach my former level. But maybe I was trying too hard. Once I granted myself more patience and grace, things turned around and my career was rejuvenated. From the day when I sat on that bench in Milwaukee to the day I retired a decade later, I won 22 more tournaments – 16 with Adam, two with Brent Doble and four with Mike Lambert. It was a phenomenally rewarding decade of volleyball, and it never would have happened if I'd abruptly walked away after just a few months of adversity.

Don Patterson

I learned an important lesson in patience during my pro beach volleyball career. My final tournament victory, which I discussed here in a post-match interview with announcer Chris "Geeter" McGee, came at age 44 in 2005 alongside Mike Lambert (right). That was eight years after I almost retired because I thought I could no longer compete at the highest level.

When I talk about the value of patience, I don't mean to imply that you should take a passive approach to pursuing your goals. Far from it. It's helpful to be hungry. It's good to push yourself. It's productive to have a sense of urgency. Still, whether you're 16 or 36 or 56, you *will* have rough patches, you *will* have slumps, and they may last longer than expected, especially when illness, injury or surgery is involved. It's important not to blow setbacks out of proportion, whether they last days, weeks or months. Figure out what you can control, and what you can do to improve and fix the issues. Stay positive and push through.

The shoulder surgery was my first major injury, but injuries are part of sports for athletes of all ages. I learned a huge lesson from that first episode, something that helped me with future injuries: recovery is *not* a straight line angling up, every day better than the last. It's rough and uneven – often two steps forward and one step back. Sometimes, it's even two steps forward and three steps back. Honestly, my shoulder didn't feel fully recovered until two years after the operation, but it felt better in each of those 24 months than in the month before.

Reflecting on my return to the court in 1997, I realize I should have shared more of my frustrations and concerns with my partner. Instead, I turned inward and clammed up. If I'd been more open, Adam might have said: "Look, I know these things take a while. Let's just ride it out." By bottling up my feelings, it made the process that much more stressful for both of us. That's another lesson learned. When things are tough and you have teammates you can trust to support you, it's big to open up with them, whether they're sport teammates or co-workers. This can actually help you do your job with more lightness and freedom, and your teammates won't have to try to read your mind.

WORST (ALMOST) TO FIRST

Adversity knocked on my door long before my pro beach career. In the early 1980s, I was one of many young players on a USA indoor national team that was extremely raw. The potential was there, and some of us would go on to play key roles in the U.S.'s dominance of the volleyball world in the 1980s, including Steve Timmons, Craig Buck, Dusty Dvorak and Pat Powers. But as we prepared for the 1982 World Championship in Argentina, we all knew there was a lot of hard work ahead if we were to compete with the top teams in the world. At the previous World Championship, in 1978, our U.S. team had finished near the bottom, 19th out of 24 teams, losing to Finland and Belgium in the process.

With that finish as our reference point, we set a goal of finishing fifth or better at the '82 World Championship. We raised our sights dramatically, for sure, but we had already competed well with top teams like Cuba and Brazil. With the players we had, we thought fifth or better was realistic. Maybe more important, we felt it was *necessary* to finish that high if we were going to be on track to achieve our biggest goal – winning a medal in 1984 at the Los Angeles Olympic Games.

Our first challenge when we landed in Buenos Aires, Argentina, for the World Championship was getting to the tiny city of Catamarca where we would be playing. It took 14 hours on a bus. We arrived at the facility just two days before the tournament, and workers were still painting the court – orange inside the lines, green outside. I'll never forget the look of our uniforms at the end of each match; they had nearly as much orange and green as red, white and blue.

Our four-team pool was really tough. Along with the Soviet Union, the reigning World and Olympic champions and No. 1 team in the world, there was also a very strong Bulgarian team. To advance to the next round of the tournament, we needed to finish in the top two. We knew that meant we had to beat Bulgaria in the first match because, at that stage in our development, we had very little hope – like most every team in the event – of defeating the Soviets.

Adding to the challenge was a noisy, belligerent crowd that threw tomatoes and oranges at us, unhappy about the Falklands War a few months earlier, when the U.S. supported the United Kingdom in its 10-week conflict with Argentina. On top of that, the day before our match with Bulgaria, one of our starters, Marc Waldie, twisted his ankle and couldn't play.

Still, we found ourselves up 12-4 against Bulgaria in the deciding fifth game to 15, which in those days was traditional sideout scoring, meaning you only earned a point if your team was serving. Nothing short of a complete meltdown could prevent us from winning. And ... we had a complete meltdown! Everything that had gone right the entire match suddenly went wrong, and Bulgaria came back to win 16-14 in the fifth.

The next night, we lost to the Soviets in three but played them tougher than any other team in the tournament did, losing three sets by 4, 3 and 2 points – 16-14 in the third. We finished pool play by trouncing a relatively weak Chile team the following day, but the damage was done. We fell into the bottom half of the tournament and could finish no better than 13th, and that's exactly how we placed. Meanwhile, Bulgaria finished 5th, the exact place we were shooting for. It was a crushing blow to our entire team, coaches included. We knew we were miles off our targeted goal.

As difficult as it was to swallow, that failure served us well in the long run. We not only learned some hugely valuable lessons from that tournament, we made crucial changes to address problems and improve our team. Looking back, I can say that I don't believe we would have won the Olympics two years later and followed it up with gold medals at the '85 World Cup and the '86 World Championship had we not suffered that 13th-place finish in Argentina.

The key lesson in this story is that improvement on the way to greatness involves evaluating what went wrong, then doing something different the next time. In the Bulgaria loss, we realized we had fallen into a trap of playing not to lose rather than playing to win. We got more conservative and error prone at 12-4, and Bulgaria took advantage of it. After suffering that loss, we pledged to play aggressively and not expect the last few points to just come our way.

Another big change we made was understanding that as hard as we had been working, we had to move the needle more. We had less than two years until the 1984 Los Angeles Olympics, so the urgency with which we trained had to go up – and it did, noticeably.

Our coaches and players learned painful lessons about our tactical weaknesses. The coaches instituted a radical new two-passer system, following the principle of featuring our best players at any given skill so they could execute that skill the most.

And finally, we added new tools to our blocking system's tool-kit. We had been repeatedly burned in the Bulgaria match by a variation they ran of the traditional X play, where the quick hitter and another hitter comes around the setter and the setter either sets the first or the second hitter. Bulgaria ran it the other way – a Back X behind the setter – and killed us with it all night. We simply weren't tactically equipped to handle it, so we had no answers.

In response, our coaches created an entirely new blocking system. We called it stack blocking. The next time we faced Bulgaria, we ran it on the first serve and Pat Powers clamped the hitter for a point. They'd never seen us do this before, and it completely shifted the balance of power between the two teams. We beat them that night, and we never lost to them again while I was on the team. We were 30-0 for the remainder of the decade. We felt like we owed them repeated doses of revenge, and we never let up. Actually, we probably should have been thanking them for the suffering they dropped on us. They made us *way* better.

BE A BEGINNER

A valuable takeaway from our experience flipping the script on Bulgaria is this: Venturing into new territory – that is, being a beginner at something unfamiliar – is good preparation for meeting and overcoming challenges. I experienced this off the court in 2003 when NBC asked me to work as a beach volleyball analyst for the upcoming Olympics in Athens. I had very limited experience as a broadcaster – just a handful of AVP events alongside Chris Marlowe, my good friend and former U.S. teammate. But this was a unique opportunity to add a fresh skill to my resume and contribute to my favorite sport in a different way, so I didn't want to pass it up.

When NBC extended the offer, my first thought was, "There's no way that I can just wing the Olympics!" Millions of Americans might be watching. To honor the event properly, I felt strongly that I owed the viewers and competitors serious effort at building my skills. It wasn't that I was afraid of embarrassing myself. I just knew that this was a huge chance to sell our sport, win new fans and teach them about the game, and I didn't want to let people down.

With that in mind, I had work to do. Lots of work. I took on the personal expense of paying for a series of lessons with a legendary broadcast coach, Lou Riggs, who had worked with Chris. At the time, I was still competing on the pro beach tour, so I would practice, quickly shower, then drive an hour – maybe an hour and a half, if traffic was bad – to meet Lou in the northern part of Los Angeles.

Lou schooled me on details big and small, everything from how to divide my time between looking at the camera and looking at my broadcast partner to how far away from my mouth I should hold the microphone – and how I should actually grip it. He also watched several tapes of my AVP broadcasts and gave me thorough critiques.

I knew I couldn't just rely on my institutional volleyball knowledge if I was going to offer enlightening commentary on so many different teams from all over the world. I had seen some others do that, and I always felt that there was something missing from their analysis. Chris and I did our homework. We talked with athletes. We talked with coaches. We collected facts, figures and anecdotes. By the time we got to Athens, we had a huge pile of note cards filled with specific background information about each athlete, especially the athletes who were likely to contend for medals. Putting in the hard work ahead of time made my job a lot easier during the Olympics. I felt prepared and confident, and when the Games were over, I was happy with the results. NBC apparently was too; they invited me back to fill the same role at the 2008 Olympics in Beijing. Since then, I have enjoyed working the booth for many volleyball broadcasts, including numerous NCAA women's championship matches alongside my good friend Paul Sunderland, another teammate from the '84 gold medal team.

Don Patterson

Working as a volleyball broadcaster, which I got to do many times with my good friend and former Olympic teammate Paul Sunderland (right), has given me the valuable experience of learning a new skill as a beginner.

It's important to note that the time you allocate to improving at any one thing has to be proportional to where that endeavor ranks on your priority list. For me, broadcasting is important, certainly important to help attract new fans to our sport, but it ranks below my strong desire to be the best possible coach I can be for our USA Women. Putting most of my time into my job and my coaching skills means I won't be as good as a broadcaster as if I did that full time. That's a tradeoff I'll make every time.

ATTACK WHAT'S RIGHT IN FRONT OF YOU

One big key to dealing with difficult challenges is concentrating on the immediate step or task at hand, not getting ahead of yourself and stressing out about the whole climb ahead. One of our 2016 and 2021 Olympians, outside hitter Kim Hill, had a really good strategy in this regard. Kim was deceptively strong, even though she's slimmer than many volleyball players. She had a reputation among her teammates as one of the hardest workers and biggest movers of steel in the weight room. People would ask her, "How do you lift so hard, so consistently?" and she'd tell them: "I just look at what I have to do next. If I have a set of eight squats, I'm just going to crush those eight." She doesn't look ahead to the 16 sets beyond that one and risk getting deflated. She crushes one, moves to the next, crushes another, moves to the next.

Focusing on the immediate task is, of course, a good strategy to apply to things outside of sports. Let's say you're just beginning to prepare a presentation for your supervisor or teacher; it's wiser not to play it out too far in your mind and go down the stressful road of thinking: "Whoa! I have *sooooooo*

much to do. I have to do this and this and this and then that."
Like Kim did with her weight workouts, just knock out one
thing at a time. For a presentation, that might mean picking
a couple of slides, finishing those – crushing them! – and then
moving on to two more the next day.

KEEP AN OPEN MIND

Another example I'll share with you on the topic of conquer-
ing adversity is a snapshot of my first foray into coaching. In
most of my years as a player, I'd never had aspirations to be
a coach. I wasn't sure I had the patience for it; in fact, I was
convinced that I didn't. But then I fell into it when our oldest
son, Kristian, decided to play volleyball for the first time as
a ninth-grader at St. Margaret's Episcopal School, a small,
private school in San Juan Capistrano, California. That year,
the varsity team had the roughest season of results you could
possibly have. They lost every match, 31 of them, and lost
every set of every match – so they went something like 0-93
in sets. In one of those sets, they were winning 20-10 and *still*
lost. It was, in a word, brutal.

As that season wound down, my wife, Janna, blurted out,
"Karch, you've got to help them!" I asked the school if I could
become involved as a coach, and they were very generous in
giving me the opportunity. My next step was to sign up for
a coaching clinic run by the legendary Marv Dunphy, who
was the head coach of our 1988 Olympic gold medal team.
The clinic ran 2½ days at his Pepperdine college campus in
Malibu. I sat near the front taking extensive notes, notes I still
keep on file. I approached it as if I knew nothing about coaching, and in many ways, I didn't. As I would soon learn, coaching and playing are very different endeavors.

To give you a little background, St. Margaret's only had about 400 students in the high school, so as most smaller schools do, they had a no-cut policy for sports teams. Everybody who tries out makes the team. That means you have a number of players who are true beginners, players who would never have a chance to compete at a bigger Southern California volleyball powerhouse like Mira Costa High or Redondo Union High or my alma mater, Santa Barbara High. It turned out to be great for me because I had to learn how to teach beginners. We had one boy on the JV team who had some visual challenges and could not pass more than two balls in a row off a wall, even after months of lessons. I realized I couldn't push a player like that too hard, and I also realized that it was important to learn as much as possible about each player individually so I could better understand how to help them improve.

Kiraly family photo

With a nudge from my wife, Janna, I took my first coaching position as the head coach at St. Margaret's High School, where two of the players were our sons, Kristian (left) and Kory (right). Among the many useful things I learned from that job was how rewarding it is to help others improve.

What I discovered in my time coaching St. Margaret's is that I *did* have the patience to be a coach. I adjusted my approach to the game to fit a much lower level of play than I had experienced in my professional career, and I found that helping others improve can be extremely rewarding. In its own way, it's as rewarding as being on the court, winning volleyball tournaments at the highest levels of the game.

In my first season of high school coaching, Kristian was a sophomore and our other son, Kory, was a freshman. The team finally won a game, and then a match. The boys went on to finish third in the league and make the playoffs. The celebration that broke out when they won that very first set was like something you'd see after a baseball team wins Game 7 of the World Series. After giving them a minute to enjoy the accomplishment, I had to remind them that if we could win one set, we might be able to win more, and we still had tons to play that day. They ended up winning the match 3-1 against a team that had smashed us the season before. It was their first win in almost two years. From then on, each year, we advanced further in the playoffs. Three years later, we won the California Interscholastic Federation (CIF) Division 5 Southern Section Championship. It was a textbook worst-to-first story.

Looking back and reflecting on those seasons, I can pinpoint several things that I believe helped turn the program around:

- **Using every minute to the fullest.** For example, instead of running laps at the beginning of practice, we played a variety of small-group games, like one-on-one short court. This gave everybody extra touches and allowed them to compete, which of course they enjoyed. The winners would move one way, to the next rung up the "ladder," while the losers moved the other, down the "ladder." It was time-efficient, fun and it transferred much more to what we were training for – controlling the ball and winning matches – than more traditional warmup routines.

- **Running game-like drills.** Rather than starting drills or points with a toss or free ball, we started most often with a serve. This prepared us for how we would have to play in a match. It wasn't nearly as pretty as starting with a coach-entered toss, but pretty isn't the goal. The goal is training to reality and figuring out the best way to play winning volleyball.

- **Feeding off success.** Once we started winning some games, I was able to stoke the team's motivation even more by simply reminding them how far they'd come as a result of hard work. In the preseason, I had purposely been understated in my messaging. Had I come into the gym on Day 1 and said, "You guys can be great," it might have sounded a bit hollow following a season in which they'd lost 93 games in a row. But once they had seen some progress, it allowed me to reinforce the idea that the improvement would continue if they stayed on the same path. On rare occasions, when a practice was falling far short of the standard we had set because of atrocious effort or focus, I would cancel the rest of the practice to get their attention and remind them that we could not afford to waste a single one of our precious minutes in the gym. I didn't make a big scene. I just said something like, "Go home, we'll see you tomorrow. And tomorrow we can use our time to the fullest."

The journey I took with the St. Margaret's volleyball team underscores a point I've become more and more convinced of over the years: Nothing that is deep or meaningful in life comes without pain, suffering and difficulty. It's true of raising children, true of becoming an elite musician, true of most any profession. And it's certainly true of becoming a great volleyball player or coach. Sacrifice, hardship and, yes, pain are part of achieving things that are lasting, worthwhile and fulfilling. I've always believed that aspiring to lead a life with as little pain or suffering as possible is a real mistake. If you avoid pain and suffering, you can get acclimated to an existence without challenges and can miss out on the growth that comes from confronting those challenges, learning new things and achieving greater goals.

This reminds me of what I've read about maintaining strong bones. To be at their most substantial, healthy state, bones need gravity even though gravity causes more pain and forces us to work harder. Astronauts who spend time in space away from gravity actually lose bone mass. When they return to gravity, the bone mass and strength come back.

This idea that *today's* obstacles will help you with *tomorrow's* obstacles was reinforced to me recently when Luka Slabe, one of our assistant coaches through the 2021 Olympics, told me about the hiring practices of a friend and former player of his at BYU, now a successful business owner. His friend makes a point of recruiting LDS salespeople who have performed Mormon missions in foreign countries. His reasoning: On a mission, you go door to door, day after day, and hear "No!" again and again. When you've heard a steady string of no's for two years, one more isn't going to slow you down or ruin your day. You become resilient and relentless. It's like you've built up armor. You get knocked down, stand up, ask again and keep asking until eventually someone says, "Yes."

In the pursuit of greatness, one "yes" is worth a thousand "no's."

CHAPTER 5
DEVELOPING WILLPOWER

If you've never seen a video of "The Marshmallow Test" on YouTube, set aside three minutes and watch. It's both humorous and a great example of the mental combat that arises within when we pit instant gratification against delayed gratification.

The subjects of the marshmallow experiment are all about five years old or younger. An adult sits them down at a table and puts one marshmallow on their plate. She tells them that they are free to eat it right away, but if they wait a while – five minutes or so – they can double their prize to two marshmallows. The adult then leaves the room while the camera zooms in close to capture the kids' facial expressions as they wait. One kid is grimacing, sniffing the marshmallow, putting it near but not in his mouth. Others are similarly conflicted. For 4- and 5-year-olds, this is a *major* challenge, although the solution was simple for one little red-haired girl. She started eating the marshmallow before the clinician had even finished explaining what would happen if she waited.

In another example, a blond kid who had not given in to temptation snapped his head around at blinding speed as the adult came back into the room.

"How'd you do?" the clinician asked, looking at the fully intact marshmallow on his plate. "Did you do good?

The boy nodded.

"Now you can have both," said the clinician, kneeling down next to him, holding up a second marshmallow.

He took it, put it beside the first marshmallow on the plate, then in one, swift, singular motion, stuffed them into his mouth. The clinician laughed.

Clearly, it was not easy for these young kids to muster up five minutes of absolute willpower in the face of an instant reward as enticing as a marshmallow, but that's the point. Willpower takes perseverance and fortitude. It is *not* easy! But if you can meet the challenge, the rewards are likely to be greater.

Studies like "The Marshmallow Test" have been followed over time and, generally speaking, they've found that kids who can delay gratification for a greater reward later on tend to go on to stronger achievements academically and in their careers. Who knows how much of the willpower they demonstrate is nature and how much is nurture, but either way, it reminds us that building up our willpower is a worthwhile effort.

One interesting aspect of developing willpower was touched on by author James Clear in his bestselling book "Atomic Habits." He wrote of a conversation he had with a top weight-lifting coach, who had worked with thousands of athletes, including several Olympians.

Clear asked the coach, "What do really successful (weightlifters) do that most don't?"

The coach responded by citing a few common factors: genetics, luck, talent. Then he said something Clear wasn't expecting. "At some point it comes down to who can handle the boredom of training every day, doing the same lifts over and over." The takeaway, Clear noted, is that "really successful people feel the same lack of motivation as everyone else. The difference is that they still find a way to show up despite the feelings of boredom."

A similar sentiment was expressed recently in a quote I read from rock musician John Mellencamp in an AARP magazine interview on "Living Your Best Life." One of Mellencamp's tips was to "keep at it," which he illustrated by saying, "Usually, I have to write about a hundred songs to get one good one. You've got to keep slugging. The problem with most people is they quit too early."

NO MARS BARS, LESS BEER

A great example of the power of willpower was seen in the 1990s and early 2000s with Arsenal, one of the elite soccer clubs in the English Premier League (EPL), arguably the top soccer league in the world. (If you're not from the U.S., you would say "football," not soccer.) Arsenal were champions of the EPL in 1991 but then went six seasons with a best finish of third. Before the 1997-98 season, French manager Arsène Wenger took over as coach, and he made significant changes to the team's off-the-field habits.

"They were very good on the pitch, but they were good at night off the pitch as well," Wenger told The New Paper, a Singaporean newspaper, referring to the players' fondness for post-game drinking sessions in the pub. "You don't suppress the beers and wine without getting some skepticism, but (the players) were very intelligent."

In other words, they bought in. With a commitment to less drinking, better fitness and improved nutrition – Wenger also banned Mars chocolate bars, which had previously been the players' go-to snack – Arsenal won the 1997-98 championship. That kicked off an eight-year run resulting in three titles and five runner-up finishes. Did willpower play a role? I think it did!

MAKE YOUR BED

William H. McRaven, a retired U.S. Navy four-star admiral, is another big advocate for the benefits of willpower. He talked about it memorably to the 2014 graduating class at the University of Texas in a commencement speech that can be found on YouTube. He describes some of the rigorous training he and his fellow classmates endured while training to become Navy SEAL officers, including spending eight hours overnight in a freezing-cold mud flat where only their heads were above the surface. What's interesting is that one of his main points is not about the toughness you develop by repeatedly enduring this type of hardship but, rather, about the benefits to be gained by performing a simple daily task: making your bed.

"Every morning, we were required to make our bed to perfection," he told the commencement audience. "It seemed a little ridiculous at the time, particularly in light of the fact that we were aspiring to be real warriors – tough, battle-hardened SEALs. But the wisdom of this act has been proven to me many times over. If you make your bed every morning, you will have accomplished the first task of the day. It will give you a small sense of pride, and it will encourage you to do another task, and another, and another. By the end of the day, that one task completed – making your bed – will have turned into many tasks completed. If you can't do the little things right, you'll never be able to do the big things right. And if by chance you have a miserable day, you will come home to a bed that is made. That *you* made. And a made bed gives you encouragement that tomorrow will be better. If you want to change the world, start off by making your bed."

I rely heavily on the idea that habits can be strung together and that one habit can be the cornerstone for many. Making your bed every day, like anything else worth doing, takes discipline. It would be easier to just leave the sheets, pillows and covers askew. In fact, there's real logic to that route. Comedian Jim Gaffigan asks, "Why should I make my bed? I don't tie my shoes after I take them *off*!" But as Admiral McRaven says, doing the little things well and with great attention to detail is a stepping stone to doing bigger things well. Once you've made your bed, you've checked one box. As you keep checking boxes, you build momentum and are likely to be that much more energized to continue checking other boxes.

To me, a big part of willpower is making a point of not cutting corners, and making your bed at the beginning of your day is putting in extra effort and *not* cutting a corner. At Santa Barbara High School, when our coach, Rick Olmstead, told us to run laps, I always challenged myself to go outside the corner of the court lines rather than cutting over them. That was literally not cutting corners, and it was a small way to exercise my "willpower muscle." If I was going to run a lap, I wanted to make it a legit one.

Another point Admiral McRaven emphasized is that making a difference in the world takes team effort. He used the example of working with his boat crew during SEAL training. To get the best of the 8- to 10-foot waves in the winter surf of San Diego, "every paddle must be synchronized to the stroke count of the coxswain, and every (paddler) must exert equal effort."

This story very much reminded me of the collective effort my high school teammates and I exerted in Santa Barbara. To get in the best shape possible during the pre-season, Coach Olmstead gave us optional conditioning assignments at the school's tiny football stadium. It took 10 triple-sized steps to reach the top, and our workout looked like this:

- 20 trips running
- 20 trips hopping on 2 feet
- 20 trips hopping on the left foot
- 20 trips hopping on the right foot
- 20 trips hopping on 2 feet, up two steps, down one, up two, down one

In total, we would make 100 trips to the stadium top for a total of over 1,000 steps. Remember, these were "optional" workouts. Any one of us could have decided we didn't want to do them and gone to the beach instead; it was only minutes away and always calling our name! But every one of us paired up with a teammate and did them religiously. We were hungry to do whatever we could to give ourselves the best chance for success during the season. It wasn't easy. But we chose the more difficult route and built up our willpower by forcing ourselves to do something that took great effort.

During the season, we had a conditioning routine that we were equally proud of. Coach Olmstead would have us run from the school gym to the McDonald's on Milpas Street, touch the wall of the restaurant, then run back. It was over a mile each way. It would have been easy for someone to not touch the wall, but I don't know a single guy who ever skipped it. On game days against weaker opponents, he had us do the same run before the match, but we were under strict orders from Coach never to run the Milpas Street route because our opponents might be driving up that street as they approached the gym, and we didn't want to have any open displays of disrespect.

When I got to UCLA, part of our warmup was an activity called the "Circle Drill," led by our assistant coach, Denny Cline, a former Bruin All-American and one of the most competitive players I've ever been around. We'd jog around the perimeter of the gym, and on regular intervals, Denny would yell, "Dive and 10!" That meant dive to the floor and do 10 pushups. As we got in better and better shape, it became "Dive and 20!" or "Dive and 30!" It wasn't long before we were doing up to 300 pushups before we even started our volleyball training, and since we did it together, it increased our willpower because we were accountable to each other.

COST VS. BENEFIT

Part of the willpower equation involves thinking about tradeoffs. That's especially important in today's world of youth sports, when athletes are forced to specialize at younger and younger ages if they want to stay competitive. They often have to ask themselves questions like, "Do I go to the birthday party?" or "Do I go to practice?" For each choice, there's a cost and a benefit. Birthday party = Having fun with friends. Practice = Getting a little better at volleyball – and also having fun, hopefully.

The more thought you give to cost vs. benefit, the more likely it is that you'll make a clear-eyed decision that you won't regret in the long run. I've seen this play out with our national team players. Choosing to continue in volleyball after college is a very big decision. It can be extremely difficult to adapt to life in different countries – China, Turkey, Japan, Italy, Brazil – and to be so far away from family and friends. There have been some really promising college senior student-athletes who have added up the pros and cons of playing at the professional level vs. retiring from volleyball and moving on to a different profession. I have complete respect for those who make the decision to retire from the sport. They have put some real thought into it, and they reached clarity, which hopefully will lead to happiness and fulfillment for them.

If you don't have clarity, it's going to be hard to do what we ask of you every day in our training gym in Anaheim, and you're probably going to have regrets or begin asking questions like:

What about family? What about friends? What about that other career? But if you've put in serious thought, and clearly understand both the costs of pursuing volleyball at the elite level *and* the costs of stopping that pursuit, it's much easier to manifest willpower and pursue your goals with conviction, whether it's on the volleyball court or in another line of work. You're all-in, so to speak, so you're less likely to waver when sacrifices are required.

Another component to willpower is developing the ability to pick yourself up off the ground after a fall. It's never easy, and depending on the circumstances, it can be extraordinarily difficult. I'm reminded of one of the toughest losses our U.S. women's team ever endured, losing to Serbia in the semifinals of the 2016 Rio Olympic Games. It was a massive soul-crusher. We had so wanted to play in that gold-medal match, and we had been working toward that goal for nearly four years. Yet in less than 48 hours, we had to come back and play for the bronze, so we needed to process our grief, work through it and then rise to the challenge of competing in another tough match, this time against The Netherlands. We succeeded in doing all of those things, and we ended up with a bronze medal. One thing that helped reenergize us after the devastating loss was reminding ourselves during a team meeting that the effort we had put in and the culture we had built was about far more than just results, wins and medals.

Our team captain, two-time Olympian Christa Dietzen, described it this way: "Medals don't define this team and will never define this team. What matters is the relationships we built, and the work that the entire team and coaching staff put in. You can't put value on that."

Christa's thoughts reinforce the idea that developing will-power is part of a life philosophy that plays out over weeks, months and even years. For that very reason, I try to practice a bit of it every week. One way I do that is by walking fast intervals up a hill by our house. I now have two artificial hips, the result of hundreds of thousands of jumps on the volleyball court, so walking works a lot better for me than running. A typical workout looks like this:

- Speed walk up the hill while pushing a bike.
- Coast back down on the bike (to prevent stress on my hips).
- Repeat 12 times at a set interval – for instance, 1:45.

The faster I make the round trip from bottom to top and back down again, the more rest I have before I start the next one. But if I go over the time mark, I force myself to get back "on track," which means less rest before the next rep.

Even though I'm not competing as an athlete anymore, I still like to test myself doing things like those hill intervals. I still need willpower to get work done in my coaching job, so practicing it any chance I get is both useful and, in the case of my walking workouts, a good way to stay more fit.

I'll wrap up my thoughts on this subject by sharing a family story. One year when I was in high school, I decided to apply a little willpower to Christmas by opening just one present per day – one on Christmas day, then one each day afterward. This drove my younger sisters, Kati and Kristi, nuts, which only made the exercise more interesting.

Well into January, I was still unwrapping presents. I found that there was an added benefit beyond strengthening my willpower. It increased my gratitude for each gift since I was able to focus on it for 24 hours.

To this day, I would still be fine opening one present a day if it weren't for one big drawback. It's rude to the gift-giver to not promptly acknowledge their efforts and thoughtfulness.

Conflicting goods. Life is filled with them!

CHAPTER 6
LEARNING FROM MISTAKES

Ever thought about how many losses occur every single day in sports around the world? With eight billion on this planet, there are millions of games and matches, some professional, most amateur, especially youth. Soccer, football, rugby, basketball, volleyball, darts, ping pong and so on. In each game, one team – or one participant – comes up short.

Drill down a little deeper and you can blow your mind thinking about how many mistakes are made across all of those competitions, whether it's by the winners or the losers. Every play, somebody essentially fails as the other team wins a point.

Of course, falling short is a big part of the journey toward mastery and greatness. The only way we don't benefit from mistakes is if we don't put them to good use by reviewing what went wrong, then adjusting our process or actions in ways that help us be better the next time.

Before we dive deeper, let me expand on a point I made in Chapter 3 – winning and losing isn't always a good indicator of how a team played. Hall of Fame basketball coach John Wooden, who led UCLA to 10 national championships from 1964-75, once said: "You can lose when you outscore somebody and win when you're outscored."

To his point, winning often masks problems that need to be addressed. Let's say a basketball team is undefeated through the first half of a season but is falling far short in some of its standards of performance. Maybe it's rebounding poorly or turning the ball over too much or producing too few assists because players aren't moving to get open. The wins may be piling up, but the play isn't as good as it could or should be.

When winning breeds complacency, it hinders growth and leaves the team more vulnerable to losses later in the season, maybe even at playoff time, when one loss ends the season – and when opponents will be the toughest. To avoid falling into this trap, it's vital for the team's leadership – coaches, captains, veteran players – to establish a culture of reflection that emphasizes looking back on each performance and evaluating both the good and the bad.

THE BENEFITS OF DEBRIEFING

With our U.S. Women's team, we hold debriefing sessions after every match, but we never do it right after the finish, when emotions tend to run highest. We want to lower the players' level of activation after matches so they can recover and get a better night's rest. Prioritizing a shower, dinner and treatments (massage, ice, etc.) sets them up to fall asleep earlier.

We've found that debriefing sessions work best the next morning, when we can have a more detached perspective on the previous day's play. The process is similar each time, and it often goes like this:

- **Open with a check against our standards.**

We have certain standards we're trying to meet, and every match against a different country provides us a chance to check our progress. For each match, we typically set several mini goals related to our standards; we make some goals really difficult, so accomplishing all at once is rare. When we reach a goal and meet a standard, it's something to celebrate. For instance, if the team has been focusing on running middles on a certain route, I might say something like: "We've been working on setting the Slide in transition, and look what we did: last tournament, we were at X level, and yesterday we achieved the Y standard. We invested significant time and effort on that in practice the last couple of weeks with some challenging new activities, and we raised our level and reached our standard. That investment you've made is paying off." Feedback like this, with stats and data to back it up, helps encourage everyone, players and coaches alike, to commit even more strongly to the process.

- **Ask: "What went well?"**

This is a chance for player and coach input. The goal is to highlight and reinforce areas where the team is succeeding to provide added incentive to keep doing more of the same.

After a particularly ugly match, it may be tough to fin
tive. But there is always one to be found. Maybe it's sor

as minimal as showing strength and resolve in the face of great difficulty. For example, when our team played China to finish preliminary action in the 2021 Volleyball Nations League, injuries forced one of our outside hitters, Kim Hill, to step in as libero. It did not go as well as she or we hoped, but wow, was she courageous in taking on that temporary role to help the team. By highlighting her strength, resolve and willingness to accept an uncomfortable role for the good of the team, it helped remind players how we can "win" even when we're outscored.

- **Ask: "What needs work?"**

In this phase, we get everyone actively thinking about what our team can do better. Maybe it's that we only got our serve in 78 percent of the time when our goal was 90 percent. Once we've identified areas in need of improvement, we have a strong foundation for creating activities and drills that will address these issues in upcoming practices, or for some correction, if our next match is imminent.

- **Ask: "What was the biggest lesson we learned in the match?"**

This is a nice blend of the previous two questions. Maybe we were down 2-0 in sets and came back and won the match in five, so the big lesson might be: "We fought back into it! What helped us do that? Let's file that info away for the next time we're down 2-0." Or maybe it went the other way; we were up 2-0 and lost in five. Then the big lesson might be, "We need to play to win and nail the door shut, not wait for the other team to give it to us."

On a side note, there may be times when debriefing sessions should be very short. For instance, if a team is playing multiple matches in one day at a tournament, it's probably best for the coach to offer some short feedback and wrap things up quickly. We look to provide the right amount of information rather than too much, especially when the schedule is busy.

Overall, reflecting on the good and the bad of our play as a team gives us a balanced approach to our preparation throughout the season. This is important because it prevents us from riding highs and lows like a roller coaster and always has us looking to get better. Like with any project in the workplace or school, success in the practice environment depends on a consistent, even-keeled approach. We strive to get a little better today, a little better tomorrow and the next day, and we try not to let the scoreboard be our only guide.

THE MENTAL CHECKLIST

Consistency is also key to moving beyond individual mistakes. We encourage players to develop mental checklists so they can execute each play with the same step-by-step process. It works like a flowchart in your brain; you ask and answer questions as the play unfolds, then take action accordingly. Here's what the order of operations might look like for our middles when our team is serving:

- **Ball: Is the opponent's first contact coming back over the net?**
    - If the answer is YES, then the middle needs to attack or play the overpass.
    - If NO, then the player moves eyes onto the setter.

- **Setter: Is the setter revealing something that tells me where the set will go before she releases the ball? For example, do hand positioning, back arch, pivot, straight arms, etc. give something away?**
    - If YES, then start to move toward the point of attack.
    - If NO, the setter did a good job of staying neutral, so wait to move until I know where it's going; this might not be until the ball leaves the setter's hands.

For a setter, it might start with:

- **Is the serve going to clip the net?**
    - If the answer is YES, stay ready to play it.
    - If the answer is NO, snap eyes to the passer, read the platform and prepare to set.

For passers, it might start with:

- **Is the serve coming to me?**
    - If the answer is YES, prepare to pass.
    - If the answer is NO, call the name of the passer, call the ball in or out and shuffle to my spot so I can prepare to be an attacker.

Being disciplined about following a consistent order of tasks will improve a player's performance since it helps that player remember to execute responsibilities and cuts down on the time it takes to make decisions. It has to be systematic.

If you're a middle blocker and you flub an overpass, it isn't enough to think, "Next time, I'll remember what to do." Better is to think, "Next time I'll ID the overpass, call the name of who should play it and be decisive." Next time might be many minutes from now, so by routinely checking things off in your head, you greatly increase your chances of executing at a higher level later in the match.

It probably won't surprise you to know that I've always been a big advocate of taking a systematic approach to each point. Honestly, I had very poor patience in my playing days if I felt a teammate had made a mistake because of a mental lapse.

One time in our training for the 1984 Olympics, I was partnered with Aldis Berzins, the other primary passer in our two-passer system and one of my favorite teammates – a really good guy. The objective was to get 10 kills in a row while hitting against three blockers and three defenders, playing just two against six. I was up first. While I hit, Aldis set and then helped me with coverage. It took me a long time, but I finally got nine kills in a row. For the 10th, I wasn't in a good hitting position, so I recycled the ball off the block with the idea that I would get another swing after Aldis or I covered it. But this time, he wasn't there. He had forgotten. The ball fell to the floor, and I fell back to zero. It took me another 40 minutes to get 10 kills in a row.

When it was his turn, he got to nine but then was blocked on his attempt to get kill number 10. I was standing in the perfect position to cover the ball, but I was still seething from Aldis' mental lapse, so I pulled my arms apart as the ball descended and purposely let it fall to the floor.

I'm sure Aldis was ready to knock my block off, and I probably deserved it, but I said, "What's the difference between you forgetting and me doing it on purpose? The result was the same. Both cost us the play."

Needless to say, I would get my point across differently today. But the message still applies. Using checklists to think ahead to your next move, no matter how little it may be, is crucial to success.

This is obviously true beyond the volleyball court, so I'll finish up with a real-world example from Jordyn Poulter, our starting setter on the 2021 Olympic gold medal team.

"I was learning to drive a stick shift in my first professional season in Italy," she says. "Driving in itself requires a high level of mental engagement and thinking ahead, let alone when you're in a foreign country. When I stalled in the middle of a roundabout, I had to put my mental checklist in place – and quickly! This was the conversation I had with myself in my head:

- "Okay, I just stalled trying to get into first gear entering the roundabout."
- "There are cars coming, my car is off, I'm still in first gear."
- "You need to turn the key and restart the car, release the clutch slower and give more gas."
- "Let's go!"

"I had my fair share of mistakes, felt extremely stupid at times and was frustrated and embarrassed. All these things come with learning new skills. The more you practice and implement your mental checklist, the easier it becomes to navigate those various situations and think ahead."

CHAPTER 7
PLAYING TO STRENGTHS, OVERCOMING WEAKNESSES

One of my most trusted mentors over the years has been Marv Dunphy, head coach of the U.S. men's national volleyball team when we won the gold medal at the 1988 Seoul Olympics and, until his retirement in 2017, the head men's coach at Pepperdine, where he led the Waves to five NCAA championships. Years ago, Marv said:

"Every great team has two or three strengths that it can almost always rely on no matter how tough the circumstances."

In my career as both a coach and player, that has proven true. On the U.S. indoor team in the early '80s, our greatest strength was our ability to side out. In that sideout era of volleyball, teams could only earn a point when serving, so this gave us the ability to wear opponents down with patience. We could be content waiting 10 minutes or even longer before scoring. We had a sideout success rate of 80 percent or above, which was a big part of why we won the Olympic gold medal in 1984. Our sideout proficiency continued to be a major factor as we dominated the world for the rest of the decade, winning gold medals at the 1985 World Cup, the 1986 World Championship and the 1988 Seoul Olympics.

After I switched back to the beach game full time in the 1990s, my commitment to siding out remained the same. I remember one tournament Kent Steffes and I played in Fort Myers, Florida, in 1996 against Dain Blanton and Canyon Ceman, a young and promising team that would win their first tournament together a year later. Sideout rules still applied, so it was a single game to 15. Dain and Canyon were up 13-8, near victory, but Kent and I bore down and just kept siding out. We ended up winning 15-13.

The next time I saw Canyon, in training the following week, he said, "Karch, I'm so pissed at you."

I laughed and said, "Why is that?"

Canyon: "Do you know how many times you guys sided out against us once we got to 13?"

Me: "No, I don't."

Canyon: "37 times in a row!"

What could I say? The importance of siding out had been ingrained in me when Canyon was still in elementary school. He and Dain both had wicked jump serves, and they could bomb you off the court when they were hot. On that day in Ft. Myers, they got the upper hand early, but our strength came out under duress. We righted the ship by focusing solely on keeping the rockets they were serving in play, then making better sets, and we sided out relentlessly. That put us in position to wear them down – it's demoralizing for any team to *not* be able to finish off an opponent – and eventually win the match.

DEALING WITH YOUR WEAKNESSES

As much as developing primary strengths are key to success, there's another big part of the equation: getting better in areas that aren't strengths. And this is where things can get tricky for coaches and players. There aren't enough hours in the day to *stay* great at your strengths and to *get* great at all of your non-strengths, so you have to prioritize, compromise and find the right balance.

Too often, teams fall short when it comes to budgeting their training and development time. Maybe they tilt too far in one direction, overtraining their strengths and undertraining their weaknesses. Or vice versa. (What part of the season the team is in should be a factor in time allocation. Generally, it's a wise strategy to work on improving weaknesses earlier in the season and to focus more on strengths as it gets later.)

A good example of "too little focus" was the experience one of our U.S. national team players had a couple of years back with a foreign club team. The coach decided that the team's success absolutely depended on being great at side-out volleyball. To this end, he allocated nearly all of the team's practice time to drills in which the A-side was in serve-receive. They just kept playing rally after rally after rally, receiving serve after serve after serve. But the team never started rallies with a serve, block and defense.

Come match time, the team was very good at siding out, as you'd expect. But they weren't good enough at it to overcome the fact that the training time allocation left their serving rough and their block and their defense poorly organized, so their win-loss record suffered. Developing one area of their game at the expense of overall balance did them more harm than good.

Another example of skewed training is the way many teams practice serving. From what I've observed, these are two of the primary issues:

1. **Gaps in training.** When our national team athletes compete on professional club teams in foreign countries, they often find that their teams skip serving practice during the week. So there might not be any serving Tuesdays, Thursdays and Fridays; then maybe they'll do a little serving before their Saturday match. Then, if they don't serve well in the match, the coach will say, "We've gotta get better at serving." But it doesn't work that way. You can't just turn a core strength on and off. Teams need to consistently work on reinforcing important skills, even if they are very good at them. Maybe it's just a few minutes each practice, but to stay sharp, it's essential to focus on that skill consistently.

2. **Static serving.** In many high school and club practices, the coach will blow a whistle and instruct, "Okay, everyone serve for five minutes." Players will then stand at each end of the court and fire away, volleyballs flying everywhere. This is OK, but it's not very game-like. When working on serving, we prefer players to do it one at a time, serving at passers and taking the time to use their full serving routine for each rep. (On the U.S. team, we receive

with three passers, so that's what we do in drills.) This comes closer to simulating match conditions, and turning it into a competition helps simulate match pressure too. Everybody is watching, and all of the focus is on the server. And the server also has to think about attacking the right space around the right passer rather than merely striking the ball and trying to get it in the court. As an added benefit, passers get lots of quality reps.

On the U.S. women's team, serving is one of our biggest strengths. Another is passing. In both skills, we have been among the best in the world. We will never have a day in our gym where we don't have opportunities to work on those core skills, and we have frequent competitions that include serving and passing so we can develop both skills in a time-efficient, game-like manner. The easiest way to do that is to start activities with … a live serve!

BIG ROCKS, LITTLE ROCKS

So how do you use time wisely so you can bolster strengths and improve weaknesses? On the national team, we organize our to-do list in what we call Big Rocks and Little Rocks. The USA coaching staff didn't invent these terms; they've been used in numerous professions. In volleyball, they were hammered home by the late Carl McGown, who coached the Brigham Young men's team to NCAA championships in 1999 and 2001 and held numerous roles with the USA program, including head coach, assistant and advisor.

The idea behind Big Rocks and Little Rocks is that they represent the things you have to work on, large and small.

Metaphorically, the Big Rocks go in the jar first, then the space around them is filled in with Little Rocks that range in size from pebbles to grains of sand. If you do it the other way round, you'll get fewer rocks into the "work" jar. We draw the rocks on our whiteboard in the gym, and we color code them this way:

- **Green Big Rock:** A strength that we need to continue investing in.
- **Red Big Rock:** Something that needs work because of its importance.

As a coach, I have my own set of Big Rocks and Little Rocks. One of my latest is to improve as a listener/communicator. For me, it's a Green Big Rock for two reasons:

1. It's a critically important skill for anyone in a leadership role.
2. It's something that I think is already a reasonable strength for me, but I want to be better at it.

In each Olympic year, our coaching staff has some really heavy decisions to make, ones that could break hearts, so I need to be at the top of my game in terms of communication. For instance, it's important for me, and for all of us on staff, to clarify processes and roles very clearly. It's a tough balance between fostering high hopes and lowering expectations. I want people to be optimistic and energized, but, at the same time, I don't want them to think they're going to get handed anything. We've all got to earn what we get.

With a goal of improving my messaging, I recently commissioned a communications coach. I'll record certain Zoom meetings, with the permission of the player, and my coach will then review the video and give me feedback. I find this to be a particularly effective way of learning. It's OK to listen to a teacher or expert talk about a certain subject in a classroom-like setting, a gym or even online, but there's no substitute for getting a performance assessment as you do the work that you're trying to improve.

After just a few communication review sessions, I had feedback that was extremely helpful. Here are two examples of tips the coach gave me:

1. **Be a better listener.** The coach pointed out to me that I was missing "tell me more" opportunities, likely because I was too focused on the list of information or objectives that I wanted to relay to the athletes rather than fully engaging in what they were telling me. Since then, rather than sticking to a "script," I'm trying to be more flexible and allow conversations to go in different directions organically. When a player shares something intriguing about her own life, I try to follow up with a question so I can learn more about who she is as a person and what drives her.

2. **Affirmations are more effective than simple praise.** Another tip the coach provided was that pointing out progress or a positive is more impactful when accompanied by examples of positive behaviors or qualities. For instance, instead of saying, "Your passing has really improved, keep up the good work," it's more effective to say: "Remember yesterday's serve vs. pass competition? You seemed to

75

know where the server was going before *she* did. You were reading the line early. And you seemed to stay composed when they were launching missiles at the end to catch up." Not only do affirmations help athletes see strengths and improvements inside themselves, but they invite further conversation instead of simple responses like "Thank you."

SET REALISTIC GOALS

I mentioned earlier that it's helpful to be realistic when setting life or career goals. This isn't meant to discourage anybody from following their dreams. It's just that I would encourage some self-reflection if you're 6-foot-4, 230 pounds and have decided you want to be a gymnast.

Similarly, coaches and players need to be realistic when setting team goals. Based on statistical data prior to the Tokyo Olympics, the U.S. women's national team ranked about sixth or seventh in the world in our out-of-system offense, so that's an area we targeted for improvement. But we know that success in out-of-system offense is more personnel dependent. Serbia, for instance, has a 6-4 lefty opposite, Tijana Boskovic, who is a prototype terminator. When they have a trouble play, they can throw a high ball to her, and she's capable of cleaning up the trash. China left-sider Zhu Ting, who is 6-6, is a similarly potent attacker.

We didn't have a player like that in our gym in the five years leading into the Tokyo Olympics. And that was OK. We loved the way we played, and we weren't just waiting around for a big, powerful hitter to show up. With that said, one of our main Big Rocks before the Tokyo Olympics was trying to improve our out-of-system offense. We wanted to go from sixth or seventh in the world to fourth or fifth. That was a good goal, and certainly an attainable one.

To make that improvement, we had to take a different approach than teams with "bigger" attackers, and there was a lesson in that. The path you take to improvement and, eventually, the road you travel to greatness isn't always the same one that others have taken. You find your own way. And to that end, we worked extra hard on all of the facets involved in scoring out-of-system points that extended beyond hitter physicality. Our setters and non-setters worked on putting up more hittable balls when we had a tough pass or a dig that

Improving my communication skills, whether in matches, practices or meetings with players and staff, was a big focus of mine during the lead-up to the 2021 Tokyo Olympics.

had to be chased down. Our hitters were always looking to get smarter with their swings.

What do smart swings look like? Here's an explanation from one of our opposites, Annie Drews, who played a key role in our Olympic gold medal performance in Tokyo:

"We learned to be creative," she says. "If I don't feel like I can have a great swing, I want to do things that are going to make traffic and cause problems for the other side. Can I take someone out who we want to take out? Or can I just blast someone's finger? I don't need to bounce a ball like some of the big, physical opposites around the world. All I need is a fingertip. That seems very achievable to anyone – doesn't matter how big you are or how experienced you are. If the set is tight, can I push and wipe it out? Can we use the block as our friend? Those are ways to make small changes to bump up (your out-of-system hitting success)."

Another way we compensated for less physicality in our attacking was asking every player to redouble their efforts on hitter coverage so they could create extra opportunities off blocked balls.

As Annie says, "If someone doesn't cover, we just say, 'Friends cover friends.' We kind of joke about it, but there's an underlying message that we can swing more freely if we know there are people who have our back."

By assigning everybody to the task, we closed the gap between our out-of-system offense and the offenses of teams with big terminators without putting it all on the shoulders of our attackers. As the saying goes, "Many hands make light work."

While we chipped away at improving our out-of-system play, we continued to work diligently to keep our serve-pass game in top form. It's in our DNA, part of who we are as a team. We understood that continuing to invest in our biggest strength was invaluable as we pursued our goal of winning an Olympic gold medal.

CHAPTER 8

CARRYING YOURSELF WITH CONFIDENCE

There's a good story involving Duke men's basketball coach Mike Krzyzewski that I sometimes share with our players. Coach K, as he is widely known, is one of basketball's most respected coaches, and he has the reputation of being a master motivator. Before retiring at the end of the 2022 season, he guided the Blue Devils to five NCAA championships and coached the USA men's basketball team to three consecutive Olympic gold medals – Beijing (2008), London (2012) and Rio (2016).

Once in a team meeting, Coach K paused a video in the middle of a fast break, pointed out NBA All Star Kevin Durant and said to one of the players, "When you see Durant with that kind of face, what do you think is about to happen?"

The player responded: "I know he's going to make the play, and we're going to win. He's projecting such optimism and confidence that I have no doubts. He infects me with that look."

The point of the story, and the reason I think it's worth telling and repeating, is that we are all capable of projecting that kind of confidence, and when we do, it bolsters us personally as well as those around us.

Of course, we aren't always confident. Everyone has doubts. I certainly do, and I'm sure Kevin Durant does. But if we can outwardly present a consistent, strong demeanor, we not only impact others in a positive way, we impact ourselves.

That last part about ourselves is a key point. If you make a habit of carrying yourself with confidence, the feeling follows. Behavior first, then emotion.

Studies support this correlation between body language and self-confidence. In a popular TED Talk, social psychologist Amy Cuddy describes a simple experiment that she and her colleagues conducted where they had subjects sit in both "high-power poses" and "low-power poses." For the high-power poses, the subjects were asked to make themselves "bigger" – arms extended, feet apart, relaxed. For the low-power poses, the subjects were instructed to become "smaller" – hunched over, legs together or crossed, arms folded.

Next, they were tested for levels of both testosterone, which is associated with dominance and power, and cortisol, which is associated with stress. After the high-power poses, the subjects had a 20 percent increase in testosterone and a 25 percent decrease in cortisol. Following the low-power poses, they had a 10 percent decrease in testosterone and a 15 percent increase in cortisol. In other words, their posture either made them more confident and less stressed or less confident and more stressed.

Cuddy, who has taught at Rutgers, Northwestern and Harvard Business School, says that "when you pretend to be powerful, you are more likely to *feel* powerful," and she explains the test results this way: "Our bodies change our minds and our minds change our behavior and our behavior changes our outcomes."

I don't want to overemphasize the power pose point. Looking the part is only one piece of the puzzle, not a substitute for developing a true inner confidence through practice, hard work and proving your capabilities to yourself. But I fully believe that you can lift yourself and lift your teammates by holding your head high and maintaining a positive physical presence. And yes, that might mean faking it a little. If you've just gotten blocked straight down to the floor, you might not be feeling great. You might be dying to stare at the floor. But think of how uplifting it will be for everyone on the court if you throw your shoulders back, look your setter in the eyes and say something like, "My fault. I'll be better the next swing. I'll stay ready!" Now your teammates are more likely to be looking forward with a we'll-get-the-next-one mindset instead of looking down, thinking, "Oh, no. We're falling apart!"

On the U.S. women's national team, as with all teams, the players have distinctly different ways of projecting strength. Outside hitter Jordan Larson, the three-time Olympian, has an intense on-court demeanor, and her face and body language reflect that. It's strong and serious. In contrast, one of our middles, former Penn State All American Haleigh

Washington, expresses a lot of outward joy, frequently flashing her big smile. Haleigh's way works for Haleigh; Jordan's works for Jordan. And both ways work for the other players on the team, who feed off their strength and positivity in practices and matches.

On the flip side, poor body language can quickly infect others and make matters worse. If your team is sputtering in a match or your work team is struggling with a project, things aren't likely to get better if you look defeated. Humans are social creatures. We're highly tuned in to those around us, so in the same way that strong or positive body language or a smile elevates the collective mood, becoming hunched and small can quickly send things in a downward spiral.

In the competitive arena, a consistent projection of strength can give you another benefit. Your appearance of confidence often deflates your opponents. For many years in my beach career, I wouldn't go to the sideline when the opponent called timeout. I was inspired by what I'd seen as a kid watching beach legend Ron Von Hagen, who would sprint to retrieve a ball at the end of a point and get back to the service line before the opposing team even had time to catch their breath. He was chiseled, stone faced and relentless, and that was intimidating to those on the other side of the net.

My method was slightly different than Ron's. I'd stand at the net after an opponent called time out, staring straight ahead, expressionless. Honestly, there were times when I was gassed and dying to sit under the umbrella for a minute to take a short rest and a swig of water. Instead, I'd just wait there until the other team and my partner returned to the court. Some of my opponents told me that seeing me do this was demoralizing to them. There I was in the hot sun, looking confident, strong and fresh – even though inside I sometimes felt the complete opposite. I'm sure they were thinking, "What do we have to do to find a chink in his armor and break him down?" There were chinks. I just wasn't exposing them.

I would seek a similar edge in practice. In the 1990s, I often trained with other pro beach players at Capistrano Beach, which is in the southern part of Orange County, California. Before practice, I'd do my jump training, and I'd often plan to finish the workout just as other players arrived for our 2½-hour practice. Sometimes, they'd ask questions. I can't say I minded giving them answers.

"How many jumps have you done?"

I'd answer without hesitation. "Three hundred – 12 sets of 25."

"With that weight belt on?"

"Yep."

"And now you're going to practice?"

"Yep."

By the end of practice, I might have been completely empty, but if I could maintain my level of play after that many hours of hard work and still look fresh, I felt it was impactful in a couple of ways:

- I was pushing myself to play good volleyball when I was fatigued, which is a better test than playing when you're fully rested. Beach tournament formats demand endurance, demand that you play multiple matches in one day, so why not practice it during the week? For that very reason, Hall of Fame basketball coach John Wooden always had his UCLA players shoot free-throws at the end of practice rather than before or during practice.

- Projecting a stronger-than-I-felt persona helped give me a psychological edge on my opponents. The way I figured it, seeing me compete fiercely after doing rigorous individual training *before* practice would plant seeds of doubt in their minds for when we faced off in weekend tournaments: "Whoa, now we have to play them and he's *rested*?!"

Looking people directly in the eyes is another useful step toward greater self-confidence, and it's a two-way street. If two people can lock eyes, there's a mutual realization that you are giving each other your full attention. This helps boost people's energy and their focus. One of our former U.S. players, outside hitter Kim Hill, is really good at this. In team huddles, she could quickly visually connect with all five of her teammates. It sent a good message that she was all in and had their backs.

A great example of the infectious nature of non-verbal communications has been chronicled by Shawn Achor, author of "The Happiness Advantage," a book that explores the edge people can get in work and life from a "positive brain." In an experiment he has done repeatedly while speaking to corporate audiences worldwide, Achor asks listeners to pair up and exercise seven seconds of discipline by looking their partner directly in the eye and showing zero emotion, no matter what facial expression the other person makes. He then asks the second person to lock eyes with the partner and smile. The results are similar 80-85 percent of the time. The partner simply "can't refrain from returning the other person's smile, and most break into laughter almost immediately."

Summarizing this outcome, Achor writes: "If these people have the self-discipline and focus to work 10- to 16-hour days, lead global teams, and manage multimillion dollar projects, surely they can handle a task as simple as controlling their facial expression for a mere seven seconds, right? But the fact is, they can't. Because something is going on in their brains that they aren't even consciously aware of."

This meshes with what I've read and experienced on the court as both a player and coach. When I flash a positive facial expression, I can induce a subconscious response in a tiny fraction of a second. Extremely tiny. One statistic I read said it takes only 17 thousandths of a second.

If, with an expression as simple as a smile, you can instantly make someone feel happier and/or more confident, it's probably a good habit to adopt.

CHAPTER 9

MANAGING LESS PRODUCTIVE THOUGHTS

What athlete doesn't dream about competing in the Olympics? Vying for a chance to stand on that podium, wearing your country's colors, gold medal draped around your neck – what could be better?

Well, *anything* could be better if you're going through the mental torture that Scottish cyclist Chris Hoy was experiencing minutes before the first qualifying round at the 2002 World Championships of cycling in Copenhagen, Denmark. In his words, he felt as if he were heading to his own execution. There was no escape. He was trapped. In those final moments, he recalls, "you don't want to be there. You'd rather be anywhere else."

Hearing this, it's easy to think that he would be a flop, happy just to get through his races and cross the finish line. Not so. In fact, just the opposite. In several cycling events, including his favorite, the Kilo, Hoy dominated for a decade. He won 11 world championships and six Olympic gold medals, including a world-record setting performance at the 2004 Athens Olympics, where he became the first British athlete to win three golds in a single Olympics since 1908. Four years later, he won two more golds at the Beijing Olympics and then won a final gold at the 2012 London Games.

So what took him from such a negative mindset to the peak of his sport? Let's begin working toward the answer by doing a little experiment. Take a deep breath, then try to clear your mind of all thoughts for 20 seconds. Ready, go!

Did it work? If you're like me (and virtually everybody else), the answer is "No!" It's very difficult – maybe even impossible – to banish every thought from your brain for even a few seconds. That's the first step toward understanding how Chris Hoy turned his mental negativity around. From experience, he knew that extraneous thoughts – in this case, negative ones – are normal, especially when your nerves are fraying in the moments before or during an important match or a big speech or any event that is meaningful to you. Actually, I prefer to stay away from the term "negative" thoughts and most often describe them as "less productive." Anyway, these less productive thoughts, in Hoy's words, are "part of the process of preparing to produce the ride of your life."

Before we go further, let's touch briefly on the science. All human beings have a small section in their brain called the amygdala, which is about the size of two almonds. The amygdala is a relatively primitive tool that has shaped our lives, and saved our lives, since humans first appeared on planet Earth some 200,000 to 300,000 years ago. It is the brain's mechanism to kick in the "fight or flight response," sending

a distress signal to another part of the brain, the hypothalamus, which then commands the body to throttle up and take
action. Back in the day, the amygdala warned us of threats
from dangerous predators. Nowadays, it also kicks in when
we're serving at match point!

The amygdala is referred to as the "lizard brain" by many who
study psychology, including Seth Godin, a bestselling author
and former dot com business executive. He has spoken
frequently about how that part of the brain can hinder our
performance by stimulating fears and thoughts of negative
consequences. In an interview with Trevor Ragan, founder
of TheLearnerLab.com, Godin was asked how the lizard brain
could be conquered. This was his answer:

"I'm thrilled you asked the question that way, because that is
exactly the *wrong* question," Godin responded. "If you're seeking to destroy, defeat, conquer the lizard brain, you will fail.
It cannot be done. Because when you try to fight the lizard
brain, you are giving it more power. Your brain is nothing
but a chemistry experiment; it's electricity and chemicals.
And when you push back on the lizard brain, when you try to
reason with it, when you say 'one more this' or 'one more that'
or 'don't worry,' it inflames and releases more chemicals. You
cannot win.

"What you *can* do," Godin continued, "is dance with the lizard
brain and realize that it is a compass, and that when it freaks
out it's telling you that you are about to do something that's
brave and bold and powerful, and you should listen to it by
doing the opposite of what it wants you to do. When we listen
to the lizard brain and welcome it and thank it for giving us a
clue, then we can use it to our own end. If you talk to the great

artists, what you see is that they do their best work when part of their brain is telling them it will never work, they'll never amount to anything, they're a fraud, they're afraid. Those are the moments when you say, 'YES! Thank you!' And do it anyway."

In Hoy's case, that's exactly what he did. When his lizard brain tried to knock him off course, he acknowledged his negative thoughts, which immediately defused and shrunk them, then got himself re-focused on his normal pre-race routine. He adjusted his helmet, gripped the handlebars, stood on the pedals, listened to the countdown and then blasted out of the starting gate and won a gold medal.

Specifically, Hoy used these three actions to deliver the performance that he had been preparing to deliver for so many years:

1. **Awareness of negative thoughts.** He noticed his lizard brain sending thoughts of terror, leading him to feel as if he wanted to escape.

2. **Understanding negative thoughts are normal.** He acknowledged that this happens to everyone because each of us has a lizard brain.

3. **Returning to the routine.** He flipped his thoughts back to what he needed to do to race his best race.

Elaborating on how he learned to flip from a negative to a productive mindset, Hoy told the *UK Daily Mail* that he sought answers by undergoing an MRI scan. It highlighted how his brain reacted when doing puzzles or calculations. When he approached the challenges with more emotion, more blood flowed to the right side of his brain. When he exerted less emotion, more blood flowed to the left side of his brain – the side responsible for logic.

"It proved to me that if I reacted emotionally, there was far more chance of me losing concentration," he told the newspaper. "So I had to tap into the logical part of my brain when I was in a stressful situation."

Developing a routine and following it is a proven way to reset whenever your lizard brain bombards you with unproductive thoughts. It could be as simple as adjusting your knee pad or giving a high five to a teammate or taking a deep breath. Or maybe picturing your dog's cute face. There are countless possibilities. You just need to experiment to find one that works for you.

For Reid Priddy, a four-time Olympian who started on the U.S.'s 2008 gold-medal winning indoor volleyball team, the routine that kept him in a positive frame of mind was talking to the volleyball. Whenever he'd go back to the end-line to deliver his jump serve in Beijing, he'd say five words out loud: "Just me and the ball." As he joked at the time, nobody has had that much conversation with a volleyball since Tom Hanks in the movie "Cast Away." But it worked. When the matches got tougher and the crowd got louder and the tension mounted, talking to the ball was Reid's way of moving from lizard brain thoughts to focusing on exactly what he needed to do in the moment.

On the U.S. women's national team, we've got a player who cues herself at the service line with a more aggressive strategy. She stares across the net at the player she's planning to serve and thinks, "I'M GOING TO BLOW YOU UP, BITCH!" I got a good laugh out of that when she first shared it with me, but it works for her, and it speaks to the fact that each individual takes their own path to mental toughness. For her, a take-no-prisoners internal message is the best way to avoid unproductive lizard brain thoughts such as, "I pray I don't miss here."

Another top athlete who improved his play by learning to dance with his lizard brain is tennis great Novak Djokovic, who is second all-time in men's grand slam titles (21) behind Rafael Nadal (22) and ahead of Roger Federer (20). Early in his career, Djokovic was plagued by an over-active mind that hindered his performance. Time and again, he would work himself deep into big tournaments like Wimbledon or the U.S. Open and then crumble at crunch time. There were real questions about whether he was going to fulfill his huge potential. He recognized that this was something he needed to address, and soon after, he began practicing meditation.

As he spent more time meditating, he noticed something. Many of the thoughts that would pop into his head were negative. Anger. Self-doubt. Fear that he wasn't good enough. Concern that he wasn't training the right way. Worries about his family. It eventually led him to the realization that he was wasting a lot of energy on "inner turmoil."

From that point on, he focused on being more mindful of his surroundings – even when negative thoughts emerged. It meant welcoming anything that entered his brain as if he were just a passive observer. It meant not dwelling on the thoughts, just letting them be. He has described it this way: "Instead of trying to silence your mind or find inner peace, you accept your thoughts as they come, objectively, without judging them, while being mindful of the moment in real time." If you do this regularly, even for very short periods of time, he says, you can "learn amazing things about yourself."

The fact that Djokovic does this in "short periods of time" is worth noting. When building habits, it's an effective and proven strategy to start with very tiny steps. Don't rush in and try to climb the mountain on your first shot! This is a point emphasized by James Clear in his book "Atomic Habits." As he points out, if you've never flossed your teeth on a regular basis, try starting with just one gap between two teeth, then make it two gaps the next day, then three the following day. The easier you make it in the beginning, the lower you set the bar, the more likely it is that you'll keep expanding on it and make it a regular habit. The same would be true for any habit. If you're adding meditation or some type of mindfulness exercise to your day, maybe you would start with only 15 or 20 seconds. That's a very low barrier of entry. Who doesn't have 15 or 20 seconds to spare?

Before Djokovic practiced meditation, his lizard brain would often freeze him up after mistakes. He was sure he couldn't hang with Federer. He was sure he couldn't hang with Nadal. But the more he worked on his mental game through meditation, the more he learned to shake off a shanked backhand or a blown serve. It wasn't that he stopped having self-doubts. It's that he was better equipped to handle them. Instead of letting a negative thought grip his mind and impact his play, he learned to acknowledge those thoughts as a passive observer, note them, then "let them slide by, focusing on the moment." He explains that "mindfulness helps me process pain and emotion. It lets me focus on what's really important." By engaging in this short routine, he is able to quickly get back to "this match, on this day," the most important thing in that single moment.

In the two examples I've shared so far, the athletes, Hoy and Djokovic, are obviously the elite of the elite. Now, I'll tell you about a high school volleyball player who fell victim to her own lizard brain at a holiday camp. In her words, here's what happened:

"The head coach asked me to demo a simple setting drill that I had done a thousand times before with my club. I could do this drill in my sleep. However, this time I was so nervous he picked me and so afraid of making a mistake that my body just wouldn't work. He asked me to set the ball to a particular location on the outside, and I just could not do it. I set it too tight, too far, too high and then too low. All the coaches and other players were watching. After four attempts, he asked someone else to demo. At that moment, I was filled with so much self-doubt and frustration, I wanted to run out of the gym and leave the camp."

I emailed this player a link to a presentation on the lizard brain that I had shared with our team, which included the Hoy and Djokovic stories. At various points in the presentation, I asked viewers to pause and either answer questions or share ideas. For the final question, I requested that they build out a scenario where they imagined having certain thoughts, noticing the thoughts, recognizing that they are normal and sharing how they would return to their routine so they could get back to "the best me possible." This was the answer that the high school player emailed back to me:

1. I am aware I am very nervous to play in the USAV Open national championship match.

2. I recognize my lizard brain is telling me I can't mess up. If I do, we will lose. I tell myself volleyball is a game of mistakes and that everyone makes them, so it's OK if I make some. I need to stay calm and focused.

3. After dancing with the lizard brain, I take a deep breath and go into my routine of focusing on the server and moving on with the next play.

With that, she thanked me for the opportunity to watch the presentation and then wrote, "I now know what to do when the game is 23-23 after I just made a mistake."

This was such a cool thing to hear from a young athlete. To me, it reinforces the notion that with a bit of knowledge and a few simple adjustments, anyone can improve their mental approach to difficult challenges. Once you embrace the idea that a noisy lizard brain doesn't have to be a precursor to failure, or even lead to failure, you're likely to move forward with more confidence and optimism.

Keep in mind, too, that staying focused on your routine and noticing and redirecting unproductive thoughts is something you can practice ahead of time, just as you would practice any other skill. Maybe it's through visualization, where you would purposely imagine making a mistake and having an unproductive thought, and then figure out the best way to get yourself back to your mental checklist. You might have a strategy for doing it that's different from your teammates, but that's OK. Whatever works. Maybe it's something as simple as laughing at the negative thought and saying to yourself, "Ha!

That old trickster, my lizard brain, just sent me an unproductive thought – just like it does to everyone. I'll get myself back to my routine now."

Another point I should make is that you might well have to adjust your routine over time. For example, some athletes find that mindfulness strategies work for a while, then become less effective. That's all part of the process. If it happens to you, experiment with some new action plans until you find one that helps you get back to a productive thought.

The final piece of advice I have on this subject is to keep things in perspective. Chances are, unless you are a brain surgeon or a pilot, whatever you're about to do is actually *not* a matter of life and death. Using volleyball as an example, there are worse things than hitting a serve into the net or setting a ball too far inside to your left-side hitter. Besides, in most instances, a major screwup turns into a funny story five years later at Thanksgiving dinner, right?

So dance with your lizard brain, refocus on the process you've worked hard to develop, then let it rip!

CHAPTER 10
BEING A GOOD TEAMMATE

Kobe Bryant was one of the most memorable visitors we ever had at a U.S. women's national team practice. The NBA Hall of Famer, who died tragically with his daughter and seven others in a helicopter accident in 2020, was a five-time NBA champion for the Los Angeles Lakers and "one of the greatest players in the history of our game," in the words of NBA commissioner Adam Silver.

In 2012, as we were preparing for the London Olympics, Kobe was kind enough to stop by our gym and chat with the team. One thing he emphasized was the importance of developing relationships. He told us that when he was still playing, he would do extensive research on players the Lakers signed, searching for articles, learning about their families, getting a better understanding of their careers, absorbing anything he could to help him establish a closer connection. He felt strongly that the better he knew his teammates, the better he could bring out the best in them on the basketball court, whether they were starters or subs.

Another point Kobe stressed is the importance of always being consistent. He described it to us in the context of why he would demand the ball at crunch time, even if he had made only one of 20 shots in the game and even if it meant being somewhat of a jerk.

"My attitude is, 'Give me the ball, and *I'll* make a decision; I do this better than you guys,'" he said. "I have no problem saying that. I'm a little bit of an asshole."

Hearing this, one of our players asked, "Do you think that shortchanges your teammates?"

"Probably," Kobe answered with a nod, and there were a few laughs in the room.

"So their response is positive when you act like that?" another player asked.

"They don't have a choice," Kobe answered. "See, a lot of times when people talk about leadership, they think you always have to pat people on the back and constantly give them encouragement. It's not like that. But you do have to be consistent. If you're an asshole, be an asshole all the time. It will make it easier for (your teammates) to adjust to how you are. But don't be one way on Monday and a different way on Tuesday. Be the same throughout and you'll all get along just fine."

A couple of thoughts on Kobe's comments:

1. The larger takeaway from his I'm-an-asshole-but-I'm-consistently-an-asshole comment is that his teammates, by all accounts, knew that he cared about the bottom line goal: getting the best out of everybody so the team could win.

2. If you choose "asshole" as your default leadership style, you'd better have the game to back it up. When Kobe talked to us, he had won five NBA championships and been the MVP of two NBA finals. You can't get away with bringing that type of attitude if you're not also delivering on the court. As his Olympic teammates mentioned in the documentary "The Redeem Team," he didn't ask anything of them that he wasn't already doing himself. One time, they returned very late from a night out in Las Vegas and bumped into him in the elevator. They asked if he was just returning too, and he stunned them, telling them no, he was just heading to his first workout. Just through his work ethic, he inspired them all to join him in early morning workouts.

Looking back on my indoor volleyball career, it's easy to recognize that I was an asshole at times too. I didn't always go to the lengths I should have to reach out to my teammates and make them feel welcome. I tended to be incredibly demanding of everybody – myself, first and foremost. My focus was on pushing us to meet the high standards we had set as a team throughout the 1980s. In the end, it worked out as well as I could have hoped, but knowing what I know now, I would have made it more of a priority to connect with teammates on a deeper level.

Kobe's point on consistency is an important one. I value consistency in the people around me, and I aspire to present a very consistent demeanor each day, whether it's at practice with the team or at home with my wife. When people are up one day, down the next – or up one minute, down the next – it can lead to everyone around them feeling as if they have to walk on eggshells. Nobody knows what to expect, and that doesn't translate to a productive working environment. If players aren't sure which version of the coach they'll see on a particular day, they have to waste time and energy adjusting to the coach's mood. That takes away from the real work of improving and preparing for the next opponent.

When I switched to the beach game full time in the '90s – and then later, when I became a coach – I developed a greater appreciation for building strong inner-team relationships and learning about people's lives outside of volleyball. Now, I view it as a key component to creating a productive environment, whether the relationship is coach to player, teammate to teammate or, in the business world, boss to co-worker or co-worker to co-worker. Going the extra mile to get to know someone sends a message to that person that they are part of the group and that they matter.

Not that it doesn't take extra effort. It does! We all know it's easier to hang out with people you already know, just like it's easier talking with old friends at a party than seeking out someone you've never met and starting a conversation. But to grow as people, I believe you have to fight "easy" and not just default to the path of least resistance. So why not challenge yourself? Next time there's someone new on the team, be the first to break the ice. It can be as simple as saying:

"Welcome! Super excited to have you here. Tell me a little about yourself."

Or maybe you go with a more specific question:

"What are three things you really want me to know about you?"

If you're a coach, you might flesh it out:

"What are three things I really need to know about you that would make me the best coach I can be for you?"

One tip I have is to start fresh with a blank slate. Don't form an opinion about someone based on what somebody else has said. I often talk to players' college coaches to get information about their volleyball skills, but I purposely avoid asking about their personalities because I don't want to be prejudiced. I prefer to learn about them with fresh curiosity, not through somebody else's lens.

DRAWING PEOPLE OUT

Not everybody is comfortable talking about themselves, so sometimes getting to know people takes creativity. A couple of years ago, when we were training for the upcoming national team season, we asked our players and coaches to share a story about a person or event that was impactful on their volleyball career. This worked out great, and it was a lot of fun. Annie Drews surprised everybody by sharing that she was a high school cheerleader. Her impactful event came when a local club volleyball coach approached her dad at a basketball game where she was cheering and asked whether she might consider trying volleyball. That set her on a path to reach the highest level of the game and win an Olympic gold medal, and we might never have known about it if we hadn't made time in our practice schedule for storytelling.

Recalling the experience, Annie says: "Answering a question like that can be big in building relationships through vulnerability. There's such a big piece of who I am that my teammates didn't know about. And then there's another piece of who I am that they know everything about. Doing things like talking about your childhood leads to some cool follow-up stories and questions. It helps you see people for who they are and why they are the way they are. The more you can know your teammates and what makes them tick, ultimately that helps you understand each other better and work together better."

As teams open up deeper lines of communication, more information can be exchanged that will help them in competition. For instance, you might discuss what you as a coach or a teammate can do to help a player if they are struggling. The first part of this would be to identify the tells. *"When things aren't going well, I do this."* Maybe it's looking at the floor. Maybe it's hunching over. Maybe it's some other less common change in body language. Whatever the cue, you need to know it when you see it.

The second part is understanding what works for the other person and what doesn't. Some players like to hear something funny to snap them out of a funk. Others might want a bit of technical feedback. Still others might respond best to constructive criticism. The more you know about the person and how they react in the moment, the more you'll be able to help them when they need it most.

A great example of a supportive teammate in our program was two-time USA Olympian Courtney Thompson, a backup setter in London (2012) and Rio (2016) who brought us a valuable combination of energy and intensity. Whenever she would sub in, she'd go up to each of the other players on the court, look them directly in the eye and make some type of physical contact – maybe a high five, maybe a tap on the shoulder. It let them know that she was there and ready to help.

Explaining her subbing-in routine, Courtney says: "I think you've got to be connected with the people you're playing with, especially the more intense the situation gets. The greatest strength of a team is how connected they are in those moments. If we foster it day to day in practice and any time we go into the match, then we can do it anywhere."

As Courtney discovered "through trial and error," you figure out what strategies work with different teammates, then react accordingly. Her roommate on road trips was often Foluke Akinradewo, a middle who was a starter on the 2012, 2016 and 2021 Olympic teams. Foluke and Courtney are good friends, and Courtney knew from experience that their communication in practices or matches should be fast and funny, not overly analytical.

"We share a similar sense of humor, and it didn't help us to get really technical," Courtney recalls. "I remember one day in practice, I set her *really* low. It's common for a setter to set the middle too low, and the middle will be saying, 'Higher! Higher!' I was so pissed at myself, but I said to her, 'You want that lower – maybe, like, under the net next time?' She laughed. The rest of the practice, she kept saying, 'Hey, set me *lowwww* here!' It gave us a point of connection and a lightness to it, which I think is helpful in those charged moments."

Like all forms of leadership, Courtney's couldn't always be light. Sometimes, it required tough love, and tough love worked for her because she had laid the groundwork ahead of time by building strong relationships.

"I wasn't afraid to be honest with my teammates, but I supported them first as people," she says. "When you do enough of that, then you can challenge their effort a little bit more. I think you can get in trouble when you challenge the effort before they know you care about them."

On a similar note, players often come to realize that *how* they share information is every bit as important as *what* they share. Three-time U.S. Olympian David Smith, a middle at the 2012, 2016 and 2021 Games who, at 35, was the oldest player on the roster in Tokyo, shares his perspective:

"Being an older guy in the gym, I often see the game differently than some of my teammates. If something happens on the court and my teammate doesn't react the way I think he should, I'll sometimes ask a question: *'What did you see there?'* Then I'll tell him what *I* saw and why that information allowed me to make the decision that I made. Sometimes another player might not know what cues to look for, but it's important to be humble in the way you communicate because it's hard for teammates to take in information if you're yelling at them and trying to cram it down their throat. You have to help them, and you have to genuinely want to help them."

Helping someone in the moment is often nothing more than reminding them that one mistake is just that – a single mistake. It's not a reason to doubt yourself. There's a good passage about this in the book "Between Parent & Teenager," written by child psychologist Dr. Haim G. Ginott. It presents a short dialogue between father and son after the son spills nails on the floor.

Son: "Gee, I'm so clumsy."
Father: "That's not what we say when nails spill."
Son: "What do you say?"
Father: "You say, the nails spilled. I'll pick them up."
Son: "Just like that?"
Father: "Just like that."
Son: "Thanks, Dad!"

Like the father in this exchange, players or coaches who are skilled at boosting the confidence of others around them understand that hitting a ball 10 feet out of bounds doesn't make you a bad player. So they say something like this: "Keep swinging! You'll get the next one!"

APPEARANCES MATTER

There's a good story from the 2008 Beijing Olympics that underscores the importance of positive communication and body language between teammates. Todd Rogers and Phil Dalhausser, who were the U.S.'s top beach team in 2008 and one of the favorites to win the gold, had a rough start in their very first match, losing to a 23rd-seeded team from Latvia. The night before the match, Phil, who is 6-9 and was one of the top blockers in the world, had participated in Opening Ceremonies. He stood for 3½ hours and didn't get back to the room until 2 a.m. His legs were dead for the match, and it showed. Todd said it was the worst Phil had played in three years.

Todd was annoyed that Phil hadn't gotten back earlier and played better, and anybody watching the match could see it in his body language. Afterward, Todd's wife, Melissa, called him out, urging him to be more supportive of his partner.

"She pointed out to me that my back was to Phil during every timeout," recalls Rogers, who is now the head beach volleyball coach at Cal Poly San Luis Obispo. "It wasn't on purpose. It's just that I put my water bottle on the left-hand side of me (instead of between them, in the middle), and that comes across as bad body language to everybody. I was obviously bitter and unhappy with the way we were playing, and as he got tooled over and over by a 6-foot guy, I was showing it – head down, grabbing my shorts. But I decided, 'I'm not going to be an asshole!' And from then on, I started putting my water bottle in the middle."

Phil and Todd went on to win the gold medal, going undefeated the rest of the tournament, including a dramatic comeback victory in an elimination match against a tough Swiss team. There's no way to quantify exactly how much impact Todd's improved body language had on their play, but one thing is certain – it didn't hurt that he became aware of his actions and made a change for the better.

IT TAKES ALL 12

One thing I've always stressed is that teams reach greatness because of the entire roster, not just the starters. In Olympic volleyball, that means 12 players. Four-time U.S. Olympian Lloy Ball, one of the top setters of his era, experienced this first-hand. In his first Olympics, the U.S. took a disappointing ninth-place finish in 1996 at Atlanta. Four years later, at the Sydney Olympics, the team did even worse, going winless and finishing last. His third Olympics was the 2004 Athens Games, and the team showed great improvement, making it to the semifinals before losing to eventual gold medalist Brazil. They finished fourth after losing to Russia in the bronze-medal match. Then in 2008, with Lloy starting in his fourth consecutive Olympics, the team went undefeated and won the men's first gold medal in 20 years.

In Lloy's view, the contributions of the subs were a huge part of the 2008 gold-medal run. For him, they set that team apart from the three previous Olympic teams he played on. Here's what he says about it:

"All the guys who didn't start on that '08 team added so much value. Of the four Olympics, it was by far the most together, like-minded, one-mission team. In '96, everybody thought they should be playing. In 2000, everybody thought they should be playing. In 2004, some players were pissed that they weren't starting. But in '08, everybody knew who the starting seven were. The other guys were fighting like hell to play, but when their numbers were not chosen (as starters), they thought, 'How can I still benefit this team?' And they all did in their own ways.

"(Sean) Rooney came in and served balls and hit some on the outside. Scotty (Touzinsky) was the most positive guy on the bench and came in with his jump serve. If we needed a faster offense, we put in Gabe Gardner. If I was hurt, (Kevin) Hansen came in. And Tom Hoff, a two-time Olympic starter, was still the captain. He would come in as a blocking sub, or he would be that stoic voice (from the bench) explaining why we should be blocking a certain way.

"Not one of those guys EVER complained or bitched about not starting, and all of them, whether they were called upon for one serve, one pass, one block or one *nothing*, were the first guys to come up and talk to us during timeouts, the first guys to tell us what they were seeing and ask how they could help. All of the things they contributed were equally important in different ways to making the team successful."

One additional point that Lloy makes is that non-starters should always be striving to elevate their status, not just be satisfied to have a spot on the team. I agree with this, and I think it's true at every level of the game.

"You want players who fight like hell in practice to take your spot," Lloy says. "They can't come to practice knowing that they're a sub and knowing that their role is smaller. They have to come in and compete and be there because they want to play, not just be there for a token trip to the Olympics. That automatically gives you the respect of the players who may be starting in front of you."

The other benefit of having players who "fight like hell" in practice is that they help raise the level of the whole gym, they keep the starters more prepared for the resistance they'll face in official competition, and they honor their teammates and friends across the net.

My final point on the teammate topic is to make sure you always allow for the fact that people act and react differently. From Courtney's perspective, the key is to keep an open mind.

"If I think a teammate is acting weird, I assume they are trying their best to figure things out – just like I am," Courtney says.

"I try to think, 'What's meaningful for her?' instead of thinking, 'This is my vision!' I'll ask questions, and then I'll try to meet her where she's at."

Bottom line, you're not going to be best friends with everybody on the team, but if you're all committed to meeting in the middle and putting full effort toward shared goals, greatness is within your grasp.

CHAPTER 11

PREPARING TO BE YOUR BEST

James Stockdale was a senior U.S. naval officer and aviator who spent more than seven years as a POW in the Vietnam war after his plane was shot down in September of 1965. During his time in captivity, he and many other captured officers were repeatedly tortured, and they had no reason to think they would get out alive. Many didn't.

Stockdale *did* make it home. He was released in February of 1973 and lived a full and productive life before dying in 2005 at the age of 81. Years after his release, in an interview with author James C. Collins, he was asked about the mind-set soldiers needed to survive such brutality for so long. Stockdale gave an answer that surprised Collins, saying the prisoners who were least likely to make it out of Vietnam were "the optimists," the ones who would say things like, "We're going to be out by Christmas." When it wouldn't happen, they might say, "We're going to be out by Easter," and when that didn't happen, they'd pick another day. The pattern kept repeating until, Stockdale said, they eventually "died of a broken heart." Summing up what he had learned from this experience, Stockdale said:

"You must never confuse faith that you will prevail in the end – which you can never afford to lose – with the discipline to confront the most brutal facts of your current reality, whatever they might be."

This quote became the central point of what Collins referred to as **The Stockdale Paradox** in his book "Good to Great." I find it highly relevant to the subject of positivity because it draws a key distinction between unrealistic optimism and a strong belief that you have the *capability* to prevail. A mix of the two is the sweet spot. I don't think it's always helpful to think, "It doesn't matter what happens today, everything will be OK in the end." And that certainly applies to sports. It's better to have a hope of winning, but not an expectation. Having lower expectations helps me get more work out of myself, toward the outcome I desire.

PREPARING FOR IMPROVEMENT

The ability to confront your "current reality" starts with preparation. Within SEAL teams and other military special operations units, this involves splitting time equally between envisioning everything that might go wrong with a mission ahead of time – and working backwards to create prevention or correction plans – and then envisioning everything going right.

In *The Talent Code* blog, author Daniel Coyle describes this as the "balanced-positive approach." In the first phase, Coyle writes, a special forces unit might spend an entire morning "mercilessly examining" every imaginable mistake or disaster. *"If the helicopter crash-lands, we'll do X. If we are dropped off at the wrong spot, we'll do Y. If we are outnumbered, we'll do Z."*

Next, Coyle notes, the team takes a break, has lunch together, socializes, relaxes, and maybe takes a nap. Then they spend the afternoon in Phase 2, vividly imagining each move going 100 percent according to plan.

"The balanced-positive approach," Coyle writes, "helps you avoid the pitfalls of positivity – namely that you get surprised and demoralized by failure – and replaces it with a preparation that matches the reality of the world and also leaves you ready for performance. Good things and bad things will happen, and you can't control either. But you can prepare."

A similar exercise to the balanced-positive approach is widely referred to as a "premortem," defined in a Harvard Business Review article by scientist Gary Klein as the process of imagining that a project has failed and envisioning all plausible reasons for that failure.

In the months leading up to the 2021 Tokyo Olympics, our team did a series of premortems. The first step was asking everyone – players and staff alike – to imagine that the upcoming Olympics turned out to be a total failure. What are all the possible causes we can imagine? How long a list can we build? I know this sounds more than a little Debbie Downer, but we found it to be a good exercise for several reasons:

1. Getting everybody's input can highlight some hypothetical issues that the coaches alone might not have anticipated.

2. It gets the entire team in a solution-based, problem-solving mode, which makes it less likely that we will panic if or when something unexpected occurs.

3. It gives everybody a license to be pessimistic. That may sound funny. But think about it. In group settings, most people are reluctant to speak too freely or in too much detail about all the things that could go wrong because it makes them seem like the voice of doom. But if that's the purpose of the exercise, then it's not only acceptable, it can also be fun – like any game or competition.

Given that all of 2021 was impacted by COVID-19, one of our what-could-go-wrong scenarios was: "10 out of 12 players get the virus and we have to forfeit two matches." A less dramatic scenario: "Everybody associated with the team – players, coaches, trainers, staff – sleeps through their alarms, and we miss a match."

In reality, both scenarios were highly unlikely. But unlikely stuff happens. Consider the U.S. men's volleyball team bus ride to the bronze medal match at the 2016 Rio Olympics. Everyone boarded on time, and off they went to the arena for the 9:30 a.m. start. Then, the bus broke down. And it was raining. So the players had to run to the arena through the downpour. It didn't hold them back. They beat Russia in five tough games and earned a bronze medal. By staying composed and adjusting, they turned the bus breakdown into nothing more than a funny story that will likely be told and retold for the rest of their lives as they reflect on a memorable day.

When you've talked through possible speed bumps ahead of time, it lightens the stress if something does happen. Let's say you happened to discuss the possibility of the bus breaking down on the way to a match. If it does break down, then you can laugh about it and say, "Hey, we got this covered. We're going to crush it!" Or maybe something happens that wasn't discussed, but you can say, "Well, we had a plan for this, this and this going wrong, and this isn't that different. We know how to problem-solve, so let's figure this out and move forward."

In the absence of some type of premortem, it may be harder to stay positive and optimistic when an unexpected challenge arises. All of a sudden, your lizard brain goes crazy and whatever has gone wrong hits you like a punch in the face. As a team, we've found that planning ahead for potential mishaps is really powerful and relieves a lot of stress.

After we've covered the premortem, our next step is to build what's called a **Risk Register**. This is a chart that lists each potential risk and projects the likelihood of it occurring (e.g., 35%). It also rates whether the impact on the team, project, etc., will be low, medium or high on a numbered scale. (Scales can be numbered any way you like: e.g., 1-5, 1-7, 1-10.) A risk register also includes a short summary (usually a couple of sentences) of how the problem can be solved and assigns an "owner" to lead the problem-solving effort.

An example of a potential problem that we identified on our Risk Register before the Tokyo Olympics was based on technology problems we had experienced in the past when playing in Japan. For whatever reason, there's often a huge amount of radio frequency activity in Japan's arenas. This can mean that our in-game video or live stats might not reach the bench devices reliably, or we could have communication breakdowns with our coaches who are giving us feedback from different vantage points in the stands.

Assessing the **likelihood** of this type of technology problem, we ranked it as a 3 on a scale of 1-4. Assessing the **impact,** we ranked it as a 1 on a scale of 1-4. Then we multiplied those two numbers to give us a **risk score**; in this case, the risk score would be 3. A score of 3 is a fairly low concern, but that's partially because we had multiple contingency plans, including:

- Using the best router we could find so it was less likely to be affected by radio frequency.
- Setting up a printer at the arena so stats or notes from our "upstairs" coaches could be printed out and hand delivered to our bench coaches if the wireless wasn't working.
- Texting information with our phones if we weren't receiving it on our tablets or computers.

By identifying potential problems and coming up with solutions ahead of time, we minimized the chances that we would be caught off guard during the tournament. It's challenging enough to try to defeat a good opponent. The last thing you want to do is compound that challenge by having staff and players unprepared for setbacks or distractions.

To give you an idea how our risk registers look, here is the one we used for the 2021 Tokyo Olympics:

Risk Category	Risk Description	Risk Controls	Likelihood	Impact	Score (Lxl)	Risk Rating	Response Type	Risk Target Rating	Action Plan	Risk Owner
Health	Bro injury.	1) Rigorous roster selection process. 2) Our primary option mid-tourney would be to switch in an OH, and in prior emergencies, most of our OHs have temporarily filled this role well.	2	3	6	Moderate	Reduce	Low	Be prepped to switch an OH in? Prepping sends mixed signals.	KK
COVID	Household member or significant other contracts COVID and the athlete is isolated due to contract tracing.	Kara will meet with athletes AND household members in April 2021 to discuss protocols for ALL.	3	4	12	High	Reduce	Moderate		KKe
COVID	Athlete or staff member has an allergic reaction to COVID vaccine and is unable to travel.	Each athlete/staff member's medical history examined prior to vaccination.	1	4	4	Moderate	Reduce			KKe
Gear	Sponsor is unable to deliver correctly sized gear in time for team departure.	We will bring extra gear. Note: Be careful not to put uniforms in hot drier that could melt numbers or letters.								JL
Health	Both setters suffer tournament-ending injuries (like MNT '85)	Alternatives: have to look at a Bro or OH to fill... would be a major scramble - most recent to have played Setter is Justine in HS.	1	4	4	Moderate	Manage			
Health	50% of players catch food poisoning.	TOC food prep and service part of COVID plan	1	3	3	Low	Manage			KKe
Other	Team can't accept AND support OG12 roster or Starting 7.	Team and Sue (Enquist) have spent tons of time working on accepting, embracing and crushing any role they're assigned.	2	3	6	Moderate	Reduce	Low		KK

Risk Category	Risk Description	Risk Controls	Likelihood	Impact	Score (LxI)	Risk Rating	Response Type	Risk Target Rating	Action Plan	Risk Owner
Other	Our 2 best servers fall into slump, struggle to serve in at 90% standard. (Slumps have occurred at some previous events.)	Choose a roster with plenty of serving skill.	2	3	6	Moderate	Reduce	Low	We would manage around this, with serving subs, and/or starting lineup changes.	KK
Staff	We invest our training time in the wrong things, and therefore arrive poorly prepared.	We are driven by data and make group decisions (therefore better decisions) about how to allocate training time.	1	3	3	Low	Manage			KK
Staff	Staff dissension over a roster or lineup decision, leading to dysfunction and poor communication during the tournament.	This has yet to happen. Still, we'll work hard to value all ideas; contributions and feedback from all staff.	1	3	3	Low				KK
Travel	Athlete misplaces passport and is unable to pass through immigration.	Players have duplicate passports that they carry in two different places – e.g., one in a backpack and one in a travel belt.	1	4	4	Moderate	Reduce	Low		JS

1	Low
2	Low
3	Low
4	Moderate
6	Moderate
8	Moderate
9	High
12	High
16	High

The final piece to our risk assessment is that we flip it around and talk about what a match or tournament will look like if everything goes right. This is a good way to end the session. After covering multiple undesirable scenarios, it's nice to finish on a strong, positive note.

WELCOME THE CHALLENGE

A favorite memory from my indoor career is qualifying for the 1985 FIVB World Cup. The year before, we had won the gold at the '84 Olympics in Los Angeles, but since our biggest rivals, the Soviets, boycotted the Games, we were eager to prove ourselves in a major tournament that included them. But first we had to qualify. In those days, the World Cup field only had eight teams, so there was only one chance to qualify. To get our spot, we would need to win our NORCECA zone Continental Championships and, in the process, beat Cuba, a very strong team.

That year, the NORCECAs were held in the Dominican Republic, and there were plenty of off-court issues to contend with. One of the biggest was the lack of running water in the half-built cement dormitories where we were housed. To shower after practice, we stood under the rain gutters in our Speedos in the afternoon rain – which came without fail every day, as did the massive mosquitos that flew around us while we rinsed off.

Despite the many challenges, we fought our way through and made it to the finals. That left us one victory over Cuba away from our desired trip to Japan and a berth in the World Cup. We started well, taking a 2-1 lead in games, but then, early in Game 4, we were hit with another challenge – a big one.

Our setter, Jeff Stork, suddenly exited the court and went to the sideline. Within our team, Jeff was known as "Lake Stork" because of his excessive sweating. It was often so bad that water would come up out of the top of his shoes and leave reverse footprints on the gym floor (dry where the shoe print was, wet all around that), and the weather in Santo Domingo wasn't helping. When he took himself out of the match, we were baffled because Jeff was the only setter we had at the tournament. Our other setter, Dusty Dvorak, the starter on our gold medal team the year before, wasn't on the trip because his grandmother had passed away.

Seeing Jeff on the sideline, a couple of our guys started yelling, "What the hell are you doing, Jeff?" But a few seconds later, he had curled up into a ball on the floor, and we realized that he was suffering full body cramps from losing so much water. We later found out that he couldn't even see straight and had to be taken to the hospital and rehydrated with five IV bags.

Our coach, Marv Dunphy, sent in a sub, Dave Saunders, but Dave was an outside hitter, not a setter.

"KARCH," Marv called out. "You're setting!"

This was a major turn of events. I hadn't set since my UCLA days, and our lineup was all out of whack; I was in an outside hitter position and we had an outside hitter, Saunders, where the setter was supposed to be.

But we didn't crumble or panic. In fact, we viewed it as a challenge, a puzzle to be solved. Could we figure things out on the fly and still play well? I think we had a healthy but realistic outlook, somewhere between "Everything is just fine!" and "There's no way we can make this work!"

Some of the early points were definitely sketchy. I put up some high balls to our opposite, Pat Powers, but they weren't nearly as accurate as Stork's sets. I tried to set Craig Buck on a Gap, and he barely got the ball over the net. Pat, never one to shy away from voicing his opinions, yelled, "Get the ball closer!" I was not particularly shy about offering my opinions either, so I yelled back, "Just hit the f***ing ball!"

Before long, I settled down, decided to keep things simple, and our offense began to click. I started setting Saunders and Steve Timmons because they were closer to me in the rotation. And they delivered. Eventually, we pulled away to win the game and the match. By not panicking, we overcame a difficult challenge to defeat a dangerous opponent and accomplish our goal of qualifying for the World Cup. It was a great blend of problem-solving and positivity.

As I mentioned in the chapter on self-confidence, different people will respond to adversity in their own way, and that's a good thing. You should be true to yourself. But in my experience, there has to be a common thread where you project an unwavering faith in the capability of your team or your teammates to meet the challenge. For some, like my former USA teammate and broadcast partner Chris Marlowe, this might be communicated through humor. Chris was one of my favorite teammates of all time, but what made him a great teammate was that *everyone* on our team felt the same way about him. He connected with each unique individual using his sense of humor, his wit, and his magnetic personality. He'd be the one making nicknames for new guys, the one getting us all to play cards, getting us to laugh at ourselves, and finding ways to make tough situations more pleasant, or even fun. When we were suffering through a difficult World Championship tournament, he was the one who convinced our head coach, Doug Beal, to have the bus stop off for ice cream on the way back from matches. Chris would get the large 70,000 peso size every time, ribbing us about our flavor choices. And our hotel restaurant served us so much soup, he turned it into fun by begging them for more! He helped make our 13th-place finish a lot less painful.

For other players, projecting that faith in teammates might come from saying something like, "I hope you get the next set. I can't wait to watch you crush it and finish this match." Or, if someone appears weighted down or overwhelmed by the moment, maybe it's making strong eye contact and saying, "Hey, you with me here? Let's go!"

ACCLIMATE TO COMPETITION

Part of maintaining a positive outlook involves not only training to *play* well but training to *compete* well. On the national team, we devote about half of our practice time to 6-on-6 volleyball – with winners and losers in each game or drill. This reinforces the standard that we play hard every time we take the court, then immediately reset and play hard again, regardless of whether we've won or lost. The more you can look at each match, game or point as a discrete challenge, the more you're likely to stay on an even keel and not get overconfident with successes or underconfident with setbacks.

This brings to mind the U.S. women's gold medal match against Brazil at the 2012 London Olympics, where I was

Hugh McCutcheon's assistant coach. We won the first set by the lopsided score of 25-11. We had played good volleyball, but Brazil missed at least a dozen serves and attacks by no more than a foot, so our wide margin of victory was deceptive. When they came back and threw a real storm at us in Game 2, we didn't mount as strong a response as we could have, and I think it might have been different if the first game had been close. Brazil won the next three games to take the match 11-25, 25-17, 25-20, 25-17 and win the gold medal. How the match might have turned out if the first game had been tight is anyone's guess, but certainly, the outcome reinforced the idea that it's very important to be wary of an easy first game and approach the next game with the same grit and determination.

One anecdote I share frequently is the 10-day slump our former U.S. libero Kayla Banwarth had in the week and a half before the 2014 FIVB World Championship. Day after day in practice, she kept losing every competition, small group, six-on-six, you name it. It was frustrating for her, to say the least, right through the last day of training. On that final day, her team played a game and lost. Then her team lost a second game. And a third, fourth, and even a fifth. As she sat out the final game of the day, her team won, and she had a mini breakdown. But then she went to the World Championship and played really good volleyball and helped us win the first gold medal at a major international tournament in the history of the women's program. It just goes to show you that when you're competing against great players who challenge you, you're going to get your ass handed to you sometimes, even if you are one of the best players in the world at your position. So try to give yourself some grace during the losses and keep at it. Losses are an essential part of life. Nothing would be very rewarding if the outcome was never in doubt. Mike Gervais, our former mental performance coach from 2013-2016, made that point during one of our first team meetings with him, saying, "What would it be like to compete *knowing* you'll win every time? Is that something we should wish for? Because there's a way that can happen…"

One player said, "How could you do that?"

Mike: "Well, I could have you play fourth-graders every day."

Obviously, winning against fourth-graders would not be fulfilling, and that's why we relish well-matched, tough competition. But that means enduring plenty of losses, and those losses can cut deep. So how do you stay positive through the sting of defeat? In my experience, the key is to focus on the fact that you are continually facing off against formidable challenges while learning and improving and

My parents, Las and Toni, have taught me many powerful lessons. They've also traveled to numerous countries to provide support, including cheering us on at the 2014 World Championship in Italy.

taking steps pursuing your own level of greatness. If you've done everything you can possibly do to perform well, you can think of that as a success, and you've also earned the right to be philosophical about a defeat.

OWN YOUR RESPONSE

A book that addresses positivity in the most serious of settings is "Man's Search for Meaning" by Viktor Frankl. It's a first-person account of his harrowing experience as a prisoner during World War II in an Auschwitz concentration camp, which was a living hell. Prisoners at these camps had all humanity stolen from them. Their identities were reduced to numbers that were permanently tattooed on their arms.

In the worst circumstances imaginable, Frankl observed one constant: Prisoners who made the best of a horrible situation generally lived longer. In other words, the one thing that couldn't be taken away from anyone at these camps was their choice of how to respond.

It goes without saying, of course, that there is no comparison between the horrors of war and sports. None whatsoever. But the idea of formulating a positive response to adversity can be applied to many areas of life, sports included. Our 2016 U.S. women's Olympic team was reminded of that by five-time Olympian Kerri Walsh Jennings before we played the bronze medal match in Rio. Between flights on her way home from the Olympics, she wrote us a note of encouragement inspired by her own experience a day earlier, when she won the bronze medal alongside April Ross.

Like our team, Kerri and April had experienced an incredibly painful semifinal loss. They were beaten by Brazil's Agatha Bednarczuk and Barbara Seixas De Freitas 22-20, 21-18, preventing Kerri from playing for her fourth consecutive gold medal. She and Misty May-Treanor had won three in a row – going undefeated in Athens (2004), Beijing (2008) and London (2012). Devastating as the loss was, Kerri and April had to regroup quickly. The bronze medal match was less than 24 hours away, and they would face the top seeds – Brazil's Larissa Franca and Talita Antunes.

Early in the match, things didn't go Kerri and April's way. Larissa and Talita won the first game and were ahead 14-12 in the second. But just when it seemed as if Kerri and April were heading for a second straight defeat, Kerri found a new gear, came back to win the second game, 21-17, then closed out the match and the bronze medal with a 15-9 victory in the third.

In her message to our team a day later, Kerri reflected on that match and urged us to "take home what belongs to you." Here's some of what she wrote:

"This match you're about to play WILL BE the biggest, gutsiest win of your entire career. I PROMISE YOU! I would never have thought that or accepted that UNTIL I lived it the other night. Gold medals are amazing. Gold medal matches are easy compared to the grit and the heart and the mental and emotional badass-ness that is going to be required of you tonight. Revel in it.

The bronze that April and I just won feels as golden to me as any of my gold medals. It was far tougher to win in many respects, and therefore it satisfies the athlete and the hunter in me more than words can say.

Breathe. Believe. Battle. Let the hurt fuel you. Lean on each other. Stay connected throughout. Whether things start smoothly and finish the same way, STAY CONNECTED. If they start wobbly and weird, STAY CONNECTED. If it's up and down and left and right and it takes you 2½ games to get your rhythm, STAY CONNECTED.

You are ALL leaders in your own way. LEAD by doing YOU with all your hearts. Focus on what's working. Keep it moving when it's working. Don't be afraid to slow it down when it's not. YOU control your own rhythm.

Kerri's words were inspirational to us and helped get us in a positive frame of mind for our own bronze-medal match, which ended up being a tough scrap with The Netherlands. We won the first game, Netherlands won the second. In Game 3, we found ourselves down 17-14, but we kept grinding, evened the score at 19-19 after a marathon rally, then closed out the game 25-22. There were no easy points for the remainder of the match, but, as Kerri encouraged us to do, we battled, believed and stayed connected. In the end, we won the match in four games to secure the bronze, making us the first U.S. women's indoor team in history to win a medal at all three Major FIVB tournaments in a single quadrennial. It was a huge feeling of accomplishment to regroup and finish on a positive note following our crushing defeat two days earlier.

Foluke Akinradewo, our outstanding middle who started again five years later in her third Olympics when we won the gold in Tokyo, sums up the experience of competing for the bronze in 2016:

"Regardless of the outcome, we knew that all the hard work we had put in and all the support we'd had for each other for all these years was what was most important. I think it really showed in the bronze medal match. There was a lot of fight, and it was for the other person. It was, 'I'm doing this for my teammates and blocking for my teammates and covering for my teammates.' That made winning the bronze that much more special."

STAYING CONNECTED

In Tokyo, en route to reaching the milestone of becoming the first U.S. women's indoor team ever to win an Olympic gold medal, we had to deal with adversity once again. During pool play, we lost two of our starters to injury: first opposite Jordan Thompson, then setter Jordyn Poulter. Both suffered ankle injuries on similar plays. Each was jumping for a block and landed awkwardly on the foot of her own teammate, the middle blocking next to her. That it happened once was strange, but twice was almost unheard of. In my 13 years with the national team as an assistant or head coach, I'd never seen that happen, and we're talking about thousands of hours of gym time and thousands of reps. But as I mentioned earlier, our team had prepared for unexpected setbacks, so it didn't knock us off our game. Annie Drews stepped in at opposite for Jordan Thompson, and Micha Hancock stepped in at setter for Jordyn Poulter. And we kept on competing ferociously.

If one moment encapsulated the team's collective optimism and support for each other, it came during our pool play match with Italy, a strong team powered by opposite Paola Egonu, one of the world's top terminators. We knew going into the match that it would be a real battle, and by then we were without Thompson, who had sustained her injury two days earlier when Russia defeated us in straight sets, our only loss of the tournament.

Italy took an 11-7 lead in the first game. On the next point, after a long rally, Egonu tipped the ball over the block, and it was covered by our libero, Justine Wong-Orantes. Poulter yelled "Mine!" and bump set the ball. Honestly, it was not a good bump set – too far off the net and not directed at anybody in particular. The players near the ball shuffled around uncertainly, and then Jordan Larson took a tentative, one-handed swipe at it with her back to the net and barely touched it. Score it two subpar contacts in a row and a point for the Italians, who now led 12-7.

Ugly plays are going to happen for any team during a long tournament, even at the Olympic level. After a particularly ugly play like that, lots of teams get small and look at the floor and skip their post-point huddle. Our team did none of that. They had what was probably their tightest huddle of the

Don Patterson

Whether the previous play went well or poorly, huddles are a great way for teammates to make eye contact, convey confidence in each other and reset for the next point.

entire Olympics, holding it for 12 seconds, looking each other in the eyes, conveying both confidence that they could overcome the situation and faith in each other.

Recovering from ugly plays is something we work on frequently during our practice scrimmages. When they happen, I'll sometimes call a timeout and have the two teams gather separately and talk about what needs to change to get us back on track. If something particularly egregious is going on, they might even discuss resetting as a whole group.

When ugly plays happen in matches, sometimes I'll call timeout and remind the players how often they've solved this problem in practice. Then, I'll turn it over to them so they can fix it.

In Tokyo, not long after our tight, 12-second huddle, we came back strong in Game 2 with a 25-16 victory. But then we hit another major speed bump when Jordyn Poulter hurt her ankle early in the third game. She had to be helped off the court, and in came Micha Hancock, our No. 2 setter, who had played very few minutes in the Olympics.

No doubt this was a big test of our resilience, and we passed. We lost that game 27-25 but kept grinding and stayed positive and eventually pulled out a five-set victory over a team that many had pegged as a legitimate gold-medal contender. That win was huge. It earned us a much better draw in the single-elimination quarterfinal. The key was just getting back to our game of making consistently good plays over and over again.

GOOD IS GOOD ENOUGH

This is a point I'd like to elaborate on. Our philosophy in the USA gym is that *great* results don't require us to always be great. We feel greatness can be achieved through a steady stream of good.

Another way to look at it is that we're not a firehose. We're more of a drip, drip, drip that puts constant pressure on our opponents.

In sports, we love to celebrate the spectacular. Spinning, thundering dunks in basketball. Diving, one-handed catches in football. I enjoy seeing those highlights as much as anybody. But the point I just made still applies: being consistently good is what gets the job done, not being occasionally spectacular.

When I was on the U.S. national team in the 1980s, we played a "friendly" match against Cuba in my hometown of Santa Barbara. To get the crowd pumped before the match, promoters would sometimes organize a "Bounce Battle," a warmup hitting contest. The objective was to hammer the ball so hard off the floor that it remained in the air for a really long time between the initial bounce and the time it descended to touch something in the gym. Air time was measured with a stopwatch.

Cuba was known for its high-flyers, so they had guys who were getting way up and crunching. On our side, the hammers were Steve Timmons and Pat Powers. Set after set, they annihilated the ball, and the crowd was on its feet with each big bounce.

Since it was in Santa Barbara, my hometown, the promoters insisted I join the contest too. Compared to the rest of the contestants, my hits looked as if they were coming out of a pea shooter. They were flat and deep and didn't produce the loud thud that accompanied Steve and Pat's hits.

For me, warmups were opportunities to take the same swings I'd need to take in the match. At a little over 6-foot-2, I knew I'd never be drilling balls straight to the floor against huge blockers, so I strived for well-placed shots that found their way through holes in the defense.

As you can imagine, I didn't win the bounce contest. Not that year. Not ever! But I was happy to surrender that title in exchange for winning a lot of real volleyball matches. Being good – not spectacular – served me well.

TEAMNESS

In Tokyo in 2021, beating Italy was a great accomplishment in itself for our U.S. women's team, but beating them without two of our starters – Jordyn Poulter and Jordan Thompson – gave us that much more confidence in our ability to compete against the top-tier teams with any of our 12 players on the floor.

More than any other win in the tournament, the one against Italy validated our belief that we were capable of "out-team-ing" our opponents, even if they had a player with superior offensive firepower. Absent a big-time terminator, we knew we had to be more closely connected to each other. We knew we had to communicate better. We knew we had to lean on our high level of trust in each other. In short, we wanted to add up to way more than the sum of our parts.

Long before the Tokyo Olympics, during the peak of COVID lockdowns, our players and staff made a concerted effort to connect with each other even though we weren't in the gym together nearly as much as during a normal quadrennial. Like many other people, our team spent a lot of time on Zoom, much of it with our Culture Coach, Sue Enquist, who helped us work on teammate-to-teammate connections.

Looking back, those Zoom chats may have been as important to our gold medal performance as the time we spent in practice.

Here's what Jordyn Poulter says about it:

"The magical thing about this team was that every single person was ready, eager and prepared to embody any role the team needed at any given time – complete selflessness and egos aside.

"As much as I'd love to say it was natural for us to arrive at that space, that would be undermining all of the work we did as a group the year and a half leading into Tokyo. The pandemic was our biggest blessing in disguise. The countless Zoom calls, tears, laughs and moments of honesty and reflection bonded us and gave us deeper trust and love for one another, even while being thousands of miles apart.

"Everyone at the Olympics can play volleyball at a high level. But the key difference that separated us was, when the pressure was at its peak, you knew that the other 11 people to your left and right believed wholeheartedly in your abilities and would have your back if you slipped up. That is the most freeing feeling as a player. When it came time for Annie and Micha to step in and embody those roles, they were ready and the team was ready to support them."

Of course, it's never easy to be on the sideline, whether it's because of health or performance. But I think focusing on a wider view of what the entire team is trying to accomplish helps you stay in a positive mindset – supportive of what's happening on the court and ready to go when you're healthy again or needed.

From Jordan Thompson's perspective, "If Annie is playing and playing well, OUR position is succeeding, and that's what the team needs. It's about putting the team ahead of what I want for myself. I know there will be times when we flip-flop. Maybe I'm struggling and she needs to go in, or she might be struggling and I'll need to go in. When you have a supportive relationship, you know that the other person isn't just waiting for you to fail. You both are aware that you're human beings. You're both going to have off days, and you're going to have their back so the team can still be successful."

Libero Justine Wong-Orantes, who was nails throughout the Tokyo Olympics and named Libero of the tournament, says this about teamness: "We elevate each other's games, and that's what being a great player and a great teammate looks like. You elevate your teammates. That's so important. Just allowing each other to feel vulnerable and speak about what you're feeling when you're not playing well. What does it take for us as teammates to lift you back up? The way we talked to each other was so open and honest."

After we won the gold, I received hundreds of texts and emails from people who seemed more impressed with *how* we won than *what* we won. Some even noted the actions of players who weren't in the game – like outside hitter Kelsey Robinson, who repeatedly held ice bags on Michelle Bartsch-Hackley's neck to help cool her off during timeouts, and gave her regular feedback about what she was seeing from the bench that might help Michelle on the court.

One text I received said simply: "Every team should study what you all looked like and how you stuck together in every situation."

Another supporter wrote: "You set a new standard for what it means and looks like to be a team."

I'll leave the final words on this subject to Jordan Thompson, who offers an eloquent summary of the team-first attitude that we are so heavily invested in:

"I want to serve my team, be humble," she says. "When you have a team that's committed to serving each other and staying in that place of humility, you are going to have success and you'll realize the value of your role even more. You realize you don't need to be the one scoring all the points. Of course, everybody would like to be the star, but there's a special thing about being a part of something that's bigger than yourself and being able to say, 'I gave it my all and I truly served the team in the best way I could.'"

CHAPTER 12
ORGANIZING FOR SUCCESS

Bad breath isn't something I like to bring to a team timeout. I look at it this way: Whatever information I might be sharing could be less impactful to the players if my mouth smells like a cow pasture.

My solution? Mentos breath mints. I stock up on them before every USA road trip, and I chomp on a couple before each game.

I mention mints not because they are a big deal in the overall scope of my job but because they are a good entry point to the subject of organization, which I believe plays a crucial role in the pursuit of greatness. The more organized you are, the more efficiency you bring to the learning process, and that leads to greater improvements in shorter periods of time.

For me, good organization starts with detailed checklists. Mentos are one of many items on my packing checklist. It's a little thing, yes, but little things matter. I know I might not find Mentos in some of the places we travel, so if I stock up ahead of time, it's one less thing to think about. The fewer little things I have on my mind, the more time I have for the big stuff.

As far back as I can remember, I've been a big believer in checklists, and even more so since reading Atul Gawande's "The Checklist Manifesto." Gawande is a surgeon at Brigham and Women's Hospital in Boston who did extensive research on how people in professions where lives are at stake use checklists to reduce errors. Take the airline industry, for example. "I got a chance to visit Boeing and see how they make things work, and over and over again they fall back on checklists," Gawande said in an interview with National Public Radio (NPR). "And the pilot's checklist is a crucial component, not just for how you handle takeoff and landing in normal circumstances, but even how you handle a crisis when you only have a couple of minutes to make a critical decision."

Gawande applied what he'd learned to the medical profession. Aided by a team of researchers, he conducted a study at eight different hospitals. Doctors were given a short checklist to complete before performing complicated surgeries. This led, in Gawande's words, to "massively better" results.

Across the medical field, many studies have reached similar conclusions. One reason checklists are so helpful is highlighted by Malcolm Gladwell in his review of "The Checklist Manifesto," which he says "honestly changed the way I think about the world." Gladwell points out that Gawande makes a distinction between "errors of ignorance (mistakes we make because we don't know enough), and errors of ineptitude (errors we make because we don't make proper use of what we know)." From that, we can conclude that "failure in the modern world is really about the second set of these errors," Gladwell writes. In other words, failures are often less about lack of effort and more about simple oversights. You might have studied hard, prepared thoroughly, practiced diligently, but that doesn't mean you won't forget one step that could lead to an unwanted outcome.

No matter how good we are at what we do, we all forget things. I know I do. I have to write stuff down. That may come in the form of a checklist, or I might make notes in a platform like Evernote – just a paragraph or two to describe something I may want to refer to next week, next month or next year. For example, when I learn a new piece of software, especially one I'll only use occasionally, I'll jot down a short checklist of how to use it. Then I don't have to waste half an hour reacquainting myself with it four months from now.

Packing for trips is another task where I find checklists to be extremely helpful, especially after the COVID lockdowns, when we found ourselves packing to travel as a team for the first time in 19 months. When you're a player or coach on an international volleyball team, you log a lot of miles, so you get plenty of packing practice. Over time, I've refined my travel checklist to a point where getting ready for a trip is virtually stress-free. To give you a visual picture, here's the list I used for the Tokyo Olympics:

Things to Add?

- White sheet + tacks/tape, for projection, if we're having trouble with meeting rooms.

- Overnight bag (eg, JPN bullet train), or small bag, one that's flat, and can fit my pillow?

Day/Days before:

- Sleep scrip – renew w doctor? Cut halfsies?
- Hair cut?
- Mentos - purchase? Reload?
- Vitamins: keep each in its own bottle, get right-sized bag to hold all (Japan Govt regs)
- Vitamins: after clearing customs, divvy out 1st 2 wks in pill organizer + pack rest in zip-locks
- Purchase - Fabreze? Liquid Detergent/ Tide Packs? Kindle Books?
- Update VS
- Copy Opponent vid locally, for Scouting on plane

Night before:

- Charge iPad; load NetFlix "sleep" shows; Harman-Kardon speaker / backup phone charger
- Shut down browsers, Restart computer - runs faster

International Items:

- **Travel:** Black USA Sweat-top, gray ABC pants, blk USA shirt, blk socks, blk pract shoes, boxers
- **Backpack:**
    - Bose headphones, Compression socks, AAA batts

- o 1st trip hydration packs, Radar gun, Elastic (for serving), Polar H10, HK speaker/charger

- o Ambien, Mentos/Gum, Travel deodorant

- o Chargers: FitBit, computer, iPhone/iPad, USB cords (2 short, 1 long)

- o Loose sweat-bottoms for travel? Only if wearing shorts

- **Loose in Checked Bag Bottom:**

  - o TripMate Nano travel router (for places w ethernet only, no WiFi) / Scented Candle

  - o Snacks / Food (tuna packs, nut butters, crackers) / Chocolate squares

  - o Hydration packets - 1 per long flight + 2 extra / Detergent packets

  - o Navy practice + Blk Game shoes (3 RWB game socks inside), Adidas belt, thongs?

  - o Gray practice sweat-top / Program Notebook / USA Trucker's Hat

  - o Pillow!

- **Big Cube:** Game Sweat-top, Game Black pants, 3 Collared Game shirts (RWN), 2 Practice shorts (GN), Jeans, Gray walking shorts, 1 pr swim trunks; 2 Laundry Loops clipped on

- **Medium Cube:** 3 USA (RGN), 2 non-USA T-shirts, 1 V-neck undershirt - rolled, Portable Light Box?

- **Small Cube:** 3 boxers, 6 vb socks (3 white, 3 black), Netgear USB WiFi

- **Toiletry kit:** Shampoo / Electric razor / Vitamins / Sunscreen / Extra floss, toothpaste / Melatonin
- Clipboard, Erasable pen set, whiteboard markers (4 colors), microfiber cloth for erasing
- *Extension Cord*, 1 outlet → 3 outlets 2-prong (prongs same size if possible), or old 1 → 3 plug
- Hand pump or ball pump, inflation gauge, extra needles, Blue masking tape
- Neck collar for sleep on flights?
- **Practice eScore Timer** – for trips that stay in one place longer (VNL, OG, etc)
- Plastic Sheet Protectors for Scout Sheets, etc

Before Bus Departs, in NTC Office:

- Wipe down computer screen w cleaner sheet
- Restock AAA batteries
- Print/Sign/Scan/Email Athlete Letters (release, etc)?
- *On bus to airport:* Call United CC, file travel notifications (Chase domestic, BoA unnecessary)

As you can see, the process begins well before I head to the airport, and it covers several time blocks:

- **Days before the trip.** This is about looking ahead. For instance, if I'm going to be on the road for nearly a month, I might need to get a haircut before I leave so I don't look too shaggy by the end of a tournament.

- **Night before the trip.** This is when I charge electronic items: iPad, Kindle, backup charger for my phone. It's a stress-reducer when you don't have to worry about low batteries on your essential devices.

- **Day of the trip.** Last-minute details. For example, on the team bus ride to the airport, I always call the credit card company to let them know which countries I'll be visiting. Just another preventive action to avoid an issue that could be harder to solve when I'm away from home.

Along with reducing the chances of forgetting something important (or even something not so important), checklists have another benefit. Each time you check a box, you get a tiny measure of biochemical joy. Progressing through a list and eventually completing it feels good – physically *and* mentally.

WALL CALENDARS AND WHITEBOARDS

Call me old school, but I like big, visual reminders of my schedule – past, present and future. The walls of my office at USA headquarters in Southern California are filled with large calendars dating back to 2013 and extending through the end of the current year. If I'm wondering how much time we trained for a certain tournament four years ago, or how many days we spent acclimating to a new continent, I just glance up from my computer.

For those who prefer electronic reminders, we also put this information on Google calendars, which are easily shared with players, coaches and staff and can be accessed anywhere we travel. I use these too, but I really value the instant "global perspective" I get from my wall calendars.

145

Whiteboards are also handy. As I mentioned earlier in the book, we use them in the gym to describe practice activities and highlight priorities (see WHITEBOARD EXAMPLES on pages 153 and 154), but we also have them in the coaches' offices. The year's entire schedule, from training blocks to tournaments to vacation breaks, is there for all to see – in bold, handwritten letters. If we're in a meeting, everybody can refer to them instantly. This way, we don't disrupt our discussion by having to look up the schedule on phones, tablets or computers.

And thanks to our assistant coach, Erin Virtue, we're using virtual whiteboards more, in the Miro platform, so we don't have to redraw plans for some of our planning.

DELEGATING

In my view, one of the most important steps to becoming more efficient is dividing your "to-do list" into two categories:

1. Stuff you do yourself
2. Stuff you delegate to others

A starting point for many people is simply buying into the notion that, much as you might want to do everything yourself because you think you can do it best, you can't. Utah volleyball coach Beth Launiere discusses this in her book "Stop Competing and Start Winning: The Business of Coaching," which she co-authored with business management consultant Leo Hopf.

"If you do a small number of important things, you can do them with excellence and bring great value to your program," they write. "If you try to do a large number of important and unimportant things all mixed together, you will get little done and add little value. As Warren Buffett, CEO of Berkshire Hathaway, says: 'The difference between successful people and really successful people is that really successful people say no to almost everything.'"

There's a sweet spot somewhere in the middle, Launiere and Hopf conclude. If you *always* say no, you could damage relationships because people "may become offended." If you always say yes, you could "lose control of your own life and work" and others might wonder about your capabilities. Why would you do so much "low-value work" if you're qualified to do "high-value work?" It's a fair question. When you're capable of high-value work, taking on too much low-value work prevents you from doing things that will have a greater impact on your team, program or company.

That said, I do make it a point to tackle some tasks that might be considered beneath a head coach's pay grade. For instance, when we arrive at airports on the team bus, I usually jump out first, crawl into the cargo area and pull bags out. It's a necessary task, and it sends a message that I think is important – that all of us, myself included, should be willing to help the team in any way we can.

Delegating is often thought to be mostly about time management, but there's another big benefit. Done correctly, it can significantly raise the skill level of everybody around you, and it can also boost their morale.

A real-life example of effective delegation can be seen in the story of David Marquet, a retired U.S. Navy captain and author of the best-selling book "Turn the Ship Around." In the late 1990s, Marquet was commissioned to take command of the *USS Olympia*, a nuclear-powered attack submarine. He spent a full year studying the sub, learning everything about it – its engineering, its guidance systems, its weapons. Part of the "Navy way" at that time was that the captain would try to learn as much about every system as possible, attempting to know as much as each of the distinct systems' experts, partially to establish respect, and partially to "show em who's boss." Weeks before Marquet was scheduled to take it over, he was abruptly reassigned to a completely different class of submarine, the *USS Santa Fe*. This happened to be the worst performing sub in the fleet. Not surprisingly, the morale of the *Santa Fe's* crew was extremely low.

With little knowledge of the new sub, Marquet had a rough start. He tells the story of giving an errant command during a routine maneuver that nearly led the sub to run aground. When he asked why nobody had spoken up, he got this answer:

"You're the captain."

Marquet decided then and there that he needed to rebuild the process. For starters, he vowed not to give any more commands. Instead, he encouraged crew members to say, "I propose we do this," to which he would respond, "Carry on!"

By getting the crew involved on an unprecedented level, Marquet learned that he didn't need to be an expert at everything. If the engineers knew more than he did about the sub's engineering, that was not only OK, it was great. They were able to step up and have a positive impact by offering a vast range of knowledge and skills that they had never previously been allowed to contribute.

The results of Marquet's new approach were impressive. No longer were crew members leaving in droves or eager to get out at the first opportunity. They stayed, and they took pride in their stepped-up roles. Their skills got better, and so did their morale. The *USS Santa Fe* went from the lowest performing sub in the fleet to the highest – all because the commander was forced to rely on his crew rather than the old-school way of having *them* relying on *him*.

Reflecting on the experience, Marquet had an insightful comment: "Leadership is communicating to people their worth and potential so clearly that they're inspired to see it in themselves."

DON'T TAKE THE EASY PATH

The challenge for some leaders is giving up control. It takes time and patience to teach, and it takes time and patience to learn. Some learn faster than others, but it's always a process, and that process can be frustrating if you already know how to do something and the other person is struggling with it.

All I can say is, resist the temptation to just do it yourself. Yes, it's easier in the short run, but down the road, you'll want people around you with a broader skill set, people who have developed the knowledge to add insightful perspectives to important decisions. And eventually, you'll want those working under you to step up to the next level. I love hiring assistants who aspire to become head coaches because they tend to be that much more motivated to work hard, learn new skills and grow. And when they do move on, it's a win-win – good for them to have reached a career goal, and good for me to know that our program helped them get there.

THE LEGROOM DILEMMA

At the crossroads of organization and delegation is one of our ever-present national team conundrums: Who gets the exit-row seats on the airplane?

As you can guess, seats with more legroom are in high demand for a team with so many players over six feet tall, so we need a plan for how to assign them.

This process begins before we even book the flight. For a recent trip to the Philippines, I sat down with one of our assistant coaches, Tama Miyashiro, and we weighed two options: non-stop with no legroom vs. one-stop with extra legroom. Tough choice, and one we decided was worth turning over to our six-player Leadership Council (LC). The initial answer came back in favor of making one stop and getting extra legroom. But then Tama and I realized we had forgotten to give the council a key piece of information. Taking the one-stop flight, we would get home 12 hours later. When the LC considered this, they reversed the decision, so we could return a half day sooner.

For future flights where we *do* have seats with extra legroom, we now have a formula for how they will be allocated. The LC came up with it after considering three possible criteria:

1. Height
2. Seniority
3. A hybrid formula that accounts for both

After some deliberation, option 2 – seniority – got the nod. Seniority has its own formula, calculated this way: Players get a certain number of points for each tournament – X for the Olympics, Y for Volleyball Nations League, Z for Pan Am Cups, etc. Once the numbers are crunched, each player is entered into a large spreadsheet and ranked.

The three potential criteria for the seat-allocation formula were suggested by the coaching staff, then reviewed by the LC. They reported back that they were good with them, but we would have been open to making changes if the council had other ideas.

Now that seniority has become our lone criteria for exit-row seats, libero Justine Wong-Orantes, a 5-foot-6 Olympic gold medalist, will get extra legroom before newly arrived 6-foot-8 middle Dana Rettke, who led University of Wisconsin to its first NCAA title in 2021. Knowing Justine, she'll almost certainly give up her seat to Dana or any of our taller players, but either way, we can feel good about how our formula was created and how the process played out. Multiple team members weighed in. A clear criterion was set. A firm decision was made.

Like Mentos, legroom on airplanes is not one of our biggest checklist items. But it's a detail that matters, and when you can handle the little things with greater efficiency, the bigger things become a bit more manageable.

WHITEBOARD EXAMPLES

On the U.S. women's national team, we use whiteboards for everything from listing team and individual practice goals to keeping stats and sharing inspirational quotes. Here are two examples:

WHITEBOARD A (p. 153): This was our Whiteboard for a USA practice in July 2019. Starting at top left, we had a step-by-step practice plan, beginning with #1 (Volley School) and finishing with #6 (Offense vs. Defense). We also included a motivational quote, four Red Big Rocks, two Green Big Rocks, and space for a "Focus of the Week" that each player could write.

WHITEBOARD B (p. 154): Another Whiteboard for that same July 2019 practice, with more details for activity #6 – Offense vs. Defense. To keep it simple, we assigned players at each position a code number. For instance, Outside Hitters 1-3 were together on the offensive team for the first game, as seen on the top line of the grid. For the second game, Outside Hitters 3-5 were on offense (second line of the grid). Other details include:

- Scoring. For this game, the offense started at zero and the defense started at 12. The winning score was 25. Bonus points were awarded for a cover followed by a kill, an out-of-system "edge tool" or an ace. Points were subtracted for a "lousy" out-of-system set, a free ball pass that was too tight to the net, an overpass or a service error.

- Final scores were recorded in the middle of the grid. Game 1 was won by the defense, 26-17; Game 2 was won by the offense 26-24; Game 3 was won by the defense, 25-15.

WHITEBOARD A

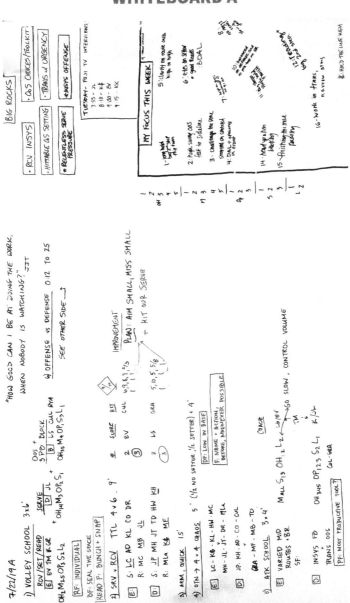

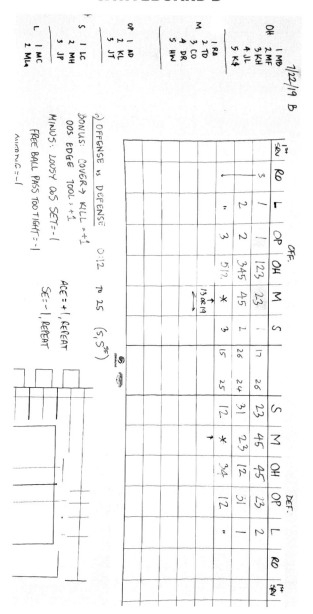

CHAPTER 13
LEARNING BY DOING

When I was 10, I read a story in *Sports Illustrated* that was a major motivator for me. It focused on some of the greatest Southern California volleyball players of the era, all of whom played at UCLA for Al Scates, who went on to win a record 19 NCAA championships in his career and was my coach when I was a Bruin from 1979-82.

Getting coverage in *SI* in the early 1970's was a very big deal, especially for volleyball players. There was no ESPN, no internet, not even much in the way of sports talk radio. Games were chronicled in daily newspapers, but the in-depth, longform stories were *SI's* domain, and if you were deemed important enough to grace the magazine's pages, you almost certainly were elite.

One player highlighted in the story was Larry Rundle, who I had seen compete in summer beach tournaments in my hometown of Santa Barbara. Learning of his diverse career accomplishments made a lasting impression on me. In 1968, he started on the U.S. indoor Olympic volleyball team that upset the Soviet Union, the world's top team. That same year, as the least tan guy on the beach, he won the coveted Manhattan Beach Open doubles title, teaming with Henry Bergmann to defeat two of the greatest players in the sport's history, Ron Von Hagen and Ron Lang. To this day, that final is regarded as an all-time classic. In speaking about it, Rundle has always been a good sport, saying he considers it a "draw" since the third and deciding game was played in near darkness.

If there was a single piece of the article that resonated with me most, it was the mention of Dane Holtzman, who held the record for being the youngest player to ever compete in a California Beach Volleyball Association tournament. He was 11. The next summer, when I was 11, my dad and I decided it would be fun to tie that record, so we entered a CBVA novice event in Corona Del Mar.

Playing that tournament was one of the huge moments of ignition in my life. We lost both matchups, but they were close. I think the scores were 15-13 and 16-14. I left the beach that day feeling empowered. Here I was this skinny kid, so far from being an adult in so many ways, yet on a beach volleyball court I could stand toe to toe with grown men.

In the coming years, my dad and I played many more tournaments. We got fifths, fourths, thirds and even seconds, but we never won. I don't remember ever being disappointed with not getting a win, nor do I remember feeling the least bit of pain after our losses. What I remember is that it was a sheer joy to compete against adults. I loved the challenge.

Make no mistake, nobody went easy on me. Our opponents did not want to lose, and they absolutely did not want to lose to a junior high school pipsqueak. They did everything they could to break me – like serving me every ball. That was phenomenal training – for volleyball and for life. Along with giving me a zillion pass-to-attack reps, it helped teach me how to handle pressure and how to become mentally tougher.

Competing against grownups had another advantage: It provided me with an inside-the-lines view of how beach volleyball *should* be played, and how it should *look*, not how it was played by other kids who were struggling to figure this game out themselves. By the time I was in high school, I had already gotten thousands of high-quality visual reps. I'm sure that gave me an edge over other players my age.

Kiraly family photo

Playing beach tournaments against grownups with my dad when I was a kid helped me become mentally stronger for challenges I would face later in life.

If there's a primary lesson to be learned from my early days on the beach, I'd say it's this: Challenging yourself by stretching your limits can give you a great foundation for future success. And not just when you're a kid. This is true at any age.

I give my dad a lot of credit. He did it the right way. He entered us in tournaments where we'd face tough opponents but not tournaments that were so far beyond our abilities that we'd have no chance of winning. We knew people who would enter the Manhattan Open just to say, "Hey, I got hit in the face by Jim Menges, and we lost 15-0!" That didn't interest us. We wanted to mix it up with good competition, not get shellacked by the best in the world. We entered novice- and B-level tournaments where we had a fair amount of success but also some failure. Occasionally, I'm still reminded of those failures when someone comes up to me and says, "I tell people 'I'm undefeated against Karch.' What I don't tell them is that you were 12 years old at the time!"

GENUINE CONFIDENCE

The self-esteem movement seems to be dying out now, but for several decades, there was a huge push to build children's confidence through praise. Much of this praise wasn't based on mastery, accomplishment or skill. It was just feel-good praise, which is hollow, even if it's well-intended. Telling someone they're great at something when they aren't may bump their confidence in the moment, but it's unsustainable in the long run. If anything, it sets them up for a bigger disappointment when they eventually learn the truth by encountering someone who truly *is* great. And maybe they already know the truth. They could be thinking, "Coach keeps saying how great I'm doing, but we keep losing, and my stats are the worst." How's that going to help a coach's credibility?

As we discussed in Chapter 6, praise can be beneficial when it's rooted in reality and balanced with a reminder to seek more growth. *"Your passing platform looks more dialed in; you were really angling to target today."* Then: *"What's been most effective for you to make that change? How can I support more of that?"* But the point I'd like to emphasize is that, in my experience, building confidence is more about doing something, not hearing about it, reading about it or watching it. I discovered this playing beach tournaments with my dad, and people in all professions have learned it by practicing different skills over and over, failing fast, then learning, failing fast again, then learning more.

This concept of learning by doing was the subject of an interesting article I read in *The Wall Street Journal* by Frank Wilczek, a physicist and mathematician who won the Nobel Prize in Physics in 2004. He started the article talking about the Beatles, who once said they really didn't "practice" per se, just spent many, many hours writing songs and performing. He included a quote from Ringo Starr: "I don't believe in practicing, really. I learned to play with a group, and I believe that I progressed more with them in five weeks than I would have in six months rehearsing by myself in an attic."

Wilczek applied this approach to his graduate thesis, saying that while many of his fellow students spent most of their time "studying, trying to ensure that they had a firm foundation before trying to build anything new," he "resolved to leap

159

right to the frontiers of research. ... I learned or improvised what I needed as I went along, made lots of mistakes – and got my thesis done quickly."

As he progressed toward the discovery that earned him the Nobel Prize, Wilczek followed a similar process with his day-to-day research.

"Hatching a new scientific concept is always an adventure," he wrote. "It's a bit like deciding to have a baby: You don't know quite how it's going to turn out. In all of my major physics insights, I got some things wrong early on and failed to nail all the easy (in hindsight) consequences. But I always trusted that good ideas, like healthy babies, would survive some blunders, grow up and thrive."

Wilczek makes a final point about embracing challenges with this quote from Danish mathematician Piet Hein: "Problems worthy of attack prove their worth by hitting back."

STRESS CAN BE GOOD

Adopting a learning-by-doing mindset can often be derailed by fear of failure and embarrassment, as we touched on in Chapter 2. To Ringo's point, it's easier to practice something alone in the attic than to put yourself out there in front of other people or in a competitive environment.

How do you avoid this fear? One way is by making a conscious effort to frame each challenge as an opportunity rather than an obstacle. Yes, you're going to make mistakes and experience setbacks, but if you can condition yourself to be excited rather than intimidated about an upcoming event, you'll prime yourself for greater success in the long run.

No doubt, some challenges you take on will be stressful. But that can serve you well, according to Stanford psychologist Kelly McGonigal, who says that stress triggers a biological response that enhances the ability to learn and grow.

"For several hours after you have a strong stress response, the brain is rewiring itself to remember and learn from the experience," she said in a 2015 interview in Stanford News. "Stress leaves an imprint on your brain that prepares you to handle similar stress next time you encounter it. Psychologists call the process of learning and growing from a difficult experience 'stress inoculation.' Going through the experience gives your brain and body a stress vaccine. This is why putting people through practice stress is a key training technique for NASA astronauts, emergency responders, elite athletes and others who thrive under high levels of stress."

Whether my early start in the game led to a biological inoculation from stress, I can't say with certainty. I do know this: I got fired up and energized by unusual challenges during my pro volleyball playing career. I remember competing in an AVP beach tournament in Seattle with Brent Frohoff in 1989. Brent was cramping and struggling with injuries, so we decided he should stand at the net while I covered the other 90 percent of the court. I chased serves from sideline to sideline that day, and, honestly, I enjoyed every minute of it. We won a couple of matches before being taken down by Mike Dodd and Tim Hovland, who were simply too good to be beaten by a team in a semi-incapacitated state.

I played that way at other times, including teaming with a friend who wasn't a pro-caliber player in a "Rated - Non-Rated" tournament. In the final, we faced Sinjin Smith, one of the beach game's all-time greats, and a very good player from Hawaii, Peter Ehrman. After a long battle, they eventually edged us. Peter, who was one of my roommates at UCLA, told me later that Sinjin had said before the match, "I think the way to beat these guys is not to serve Karch on the sidelines. The harder you make him work, the better he's going to be. Let's just serve him right in the middle of the court where he's standing." I liked hearing this. It validated what I have always aimed to do: Welcome challenges and push my limits.

With the women's national team, we pushed the limits in a different way, working with Navy SEALs the summer of 2018 to create an experience that would underscore the idea that we all are capable of doing more than we think we are. Our instructions from the SEALs were simple: Show up on a Monday night with a couple of changes of undergarments. Once we got there, the "fun" began. They immediately began crushing us with full-sprint relay races mixed with other physical challenges – like pushups. We started around 10:30 p.m., which is already pushing my bedtime, then were driven to Joshua Tree, a national park in the desert east of Los Angeles. We hiked in the dark for hours until we reached the peak of a small mountain. Our reward was seeing a beautiful sunrise. The rest of the day consisted of more hiking, other physical challenges, then dinner. Just when we thought we were done for the day, one of the SEALs shouted:

"Pack it up and get in the vans!"

None of us could believe it. Our work was *not* done. After a short ride, we hiked up an even taller mountain than the first one. This time, we had to carry an incredibly thick rope and stay connected to each other. We reached the peak of around 3,000 feet in time to see a nice sunset. We then rode back to camp and finally – finally! – got to crawl into our sleeping bags.

At the end of this incredibly long day, Jimmy Stitz, our athletic performance coach at the time, looked at his watch and noted that we had covered 19 miles in less than 24 hours. I was stunned. This was before my second hip replacement. I wasn't exactly hobbling, but I wasn't 100 percent either. If you asked me beforehand if I could walk that much in one day, I would have said, "No way!" I had known that I could push my limits on the volleyball court. This experience reminded me – and reminded everyone in our program who participated – that we could also push our limits outside the lines, that we were capable of so much more than we thought.

When you ponder it, taking a just-do-it approach and confronting unknown challenges builds your psyche much in the same way that a good weight workout builds your muscles. The more "workouts" you do, the stronger you get. The stronger you get, the *better* you get – and the more you enjoy the experience. It's a win on all levels. So why not go for it?

CHAPTER 14
INSPIRATION

I'm a quote collector. Whenever I find one I like, I add it to a master list on my computer. It might be from a Greek philosopher who lived 2,000 years ago, or it might be from a coach, teacher or businessperson who is still alive and working today. The more variety, the better.

The way I look at it, there's not enough time in an individual's life to make every mistake and gain knowledge from it, so acquiring wisdom from others is necessary for personal growth. You learn from their solutions *and* from their setbacks. And quotes make this learning easy because, well, they're short. The time investment is minimal.

I make a habit of reading through my quote list once or twice a year, and I will often pick one and write it on the whiteboard so the team can talk about it for a few minutes before practice. It's a nice way to get people thinking, and the quotes relate very strongly to themes that we work on regularly.

In this chapter, I've shared some of my favorite quotes. I hope they will resonate with you the way they resonate with me, and I also hope that they will encourage you to make your own quote list. It's nice to have bite-sized inspiration at your fingertips.

WORDS OF WISDOM

"It is not the critic who counts; not the man who points out how the strong man stumbles, or where the doer of deeds could have done them better. The credit belongs to the man who is actually in the arena, whose face is marred by dust and sweat and blood; who strives valiantly; who errs, who comes up short again and again, because there is no effort without error and shortcoming; but who does actually strive to do the deeds; who knows great enthusiasms, the great devotions; who spends himself in a worthy cause; who at the best knows in the end the triumph of high achievement, and who at the worst, if he fails, at least fails while daring greatly, so that his place shall never be with those cold and timid souls who neither know victory nor defeat."
  – Theodore Roosevelt, 26th U.S. president

"If you don't make mistakes, you're not working on hard enough problems – and that's a big mistake."
  – Frank Wilczek, physicist, Nobel Prize laureate

"The key to (making a good peanut butter and jelly sandwich) is to spread the peanut butter on both sides of the bread so the jelly doesn't leak through."
  – Bill Belichick, New England Patriots Head Coach

"Sometimes magic is just someone spending more time on something than anyone else might reasonably expect."
 – **Teller, magician**

"We do not choose to be born. We do not choose our parents. We do not choose our historical epoch, or the country of our birth, or the immediate circumstances of our upbringing. We do not, most of us, choose to die; nor do we choose the time or conditions of our death. But within all this realm of choice-lessness, we do choose how we shall live: courageously or in cowardice, honorably or dishonorably, with purpose or in drift. We decide what is important and what is trivial in life. We decide that what makes us significant is either what we do or what we refuse to do. But no matter how indifferent the universe may be to our choices and decisions, these choices and decisions are ours to make. We decide. We choose. And as we decide and choose, so are our lives formed."
 – **Joseph Epstein, author**

"Don't look at the wall."
 – **Mario Andretti, auto racing driver, when asked for his best tip to young drivers**

"Courage is showing up when you can't (completely) predict or control the outcome. If you're going to dare greatly, you're going to get your ass kicked at some point. If you choose courage, you will absolutely know failure, disappointment, setback, even heartbreak. That's why we call it courage. That's why it's so rare. Sometimes the bravest and most important thing you can do is show up."
 – **Brené Brown, clinical social worker, author, lecturer**

"The only way to discover the limits of the possible is to go beyond them into the impossible."

– Arthur C. Clarke, science fiction author

"We believe there is no good explanation or justification for why you have to be a jerk to be a good athlete, so we just won't have that kind of thing on our team. You have to get along with everyone."

– Kjetil Jansrud, Olympic gold medalist on the Norwegian Alpine Ski Team

"If you're not making mistakes, you're not doing anything. The doer makes mistakes. However, be sure your mistakes are not the result of poor preparation or sloppy execution."

– John Wooden, Hall of Fame basketball coach

"When you expect results to occur and they don't magically appear, your mind assumes nothing is happening. In reality, a lot is actually happening. You just don't see it."

– John Brubaker, leadership coach and author

"The best teachers are those who show you where to look but not what to see."

– Alexandra Trentor, teacher

"I've learned that people will forget what you said, people will forget what you did, but people will never forget how you made them feel."

– Maya Angelou, author, civil rights activist

"Where all think alike, no one thinks very much."

– Walter Lippmann, author

"Your success or failure at anything ultimately depends on your ability to solve problems, so don't become a robot. … Thinking for yourself helps develop your powers of judgment."
  – Wynton Marsalis, jazz musician

"If you hear that someone is speaking ill of you, instead of trying to defend yourself you should say: 'He obviously does not know me very well, since there are so many other faults he could have mentioned.'"
  – Epictetus, Greek philosopher

"Enjoy the little things, for one day you may look back and realize they were the big things."
  – Robert Brault, author

"Everybody has a plan until you get punched in the mouth."
  – Mike Tyson, champion heavyweight boxer

"This thing they call 'failure' is not the falling down, it's the staying down."
  – Mary Pickford, film actress and producer

"You might not be an incredible athlete, but if you never miss workouts, then you'll be better than most because you are doing the work. You might not be a savvy businessperson, but if you make a point to serve your customers every single day, then you'll be better than most because you are doing the work. The single greatest skill in any endeavor is doing the work."
  – James Clear, author

"An adventure is nothing more than a crisis that you accept. Put another way, a crisis is nothing but an adventure against which you try to defend yourself. Adventure begins the moment you leave your comfort zone. You say goodbye to habits and security and use your questions and doubts to stimulate creativity ... You don't need a spectacular aircraft. All you need is to switch jobs, move to a new place or learn a new language ... We should never underestimate the small adventures we encounter every day."

- **Bertrand Piccard, first person to complete a non-stop flight around the globe in a hot air balloon**

"If you only go through life doing stuff that's easy, shame on you."

- **Carol Dweck, psychologist, author**

"It is rarely a mysterious technique that drives us to the top, but rather a profound mastery of what may well be a basic skill set."

- **Joshua Waitzkin, chess champion, martial arts competitor, author**

"People do not decide their futures, they decide their habits and their habits decide their futures."

- **F. Matthias Alexander, author, educator, actor**

"You can either be judged because you created something or ignored because you left your greatness inside of you."

- **James Clear, author**

"Success consists of going from failure to failure without losing your enthusiasm."

- **Winston Churchill, Prime Minister of the United Kingdom (1940-45, 1951-55)**

CHAPTER 15

GO FOR IT!

It is my great hope that you've found some nuggets in this book, some impactful ideas that might help you pursue a better version of yourself in whatever area of life you choose – as a teammate, as an athlete, as a leader … as anything, really. There are many words that can describe that pursuit: mastery, excellence, flourishing, thriving, and greatness, among others. Whatever word resonates most with you, it helps to remember a few things.

1. If you've found some ideas you'd like to pursue, start by keeping your focus narrow – on just one or two concepts. If you're trying to get better at 5 or 10 things, you're very likely not getting better at any of them.

2. The word you choose to signify that pursuit does not at all imply having to "win it all" – e.g., a state championship or NCAA title or Olympic gold medal. It means consistently applying yourself toward "better," so after weeks, months

and years, you can see the old you in the rearview mirror and detect real and durable improvement.

3. As touched on throughout this book (including certain quotes in the previous chapter), that pursuit will not be a steady path with zero setbacks. All-time NBA great Michael Jordan made a famous Nike commercial where he recounted all the game-winning shots he *missed*. While the shots he made caught most of our attention, it's helpful and comforting to remember his failures. I entered hundreds of beach tournaments, and lost more – over 150 at the Open level alone – than I won. Those setbacks and failures, that suffering, help us learn about ourselves, and help inoculate us for the inevitable setbacks that are part of life.

4. The benefits of becoming a better "improver" and "learner" can be amplified and applied in *all* areas of your life.

With that, I wish you the best of luck and cheer you on as you pursue a rewarding path for yourself and … Go for it!

NOTES

INTRODUCTION

Page 1 "prehistoric people had the exact same natural resources that we have now": Thomas Sowell, *Knowledge and Decisions* (Basic Books)

CHAPTER 1

Page 6 "Joe DiMaggio ... natural hitter": James Clear, "The Myth of Deliberate Practice," https://jamesclear.com/deliberate-practice-myth

CHAPTER 2

Page 17 "Belichick appalled at players not finishing conditioning drills": David Halberstam, *The Education of a Coach* (Hachette Books)

CHAPTER 3

Page 19 "deliberate practice": Anders Ericsson and Robert Pool, *Peak: Secrets from the New Science of Expertise* (Eamon Dolan/HMH)

Page 19 "10,000 hours": Malcolm Gladwell, *Outliers: The Story of Success* (Little, Brown and Company)

Page 25 "purposeful practice": Timothy D. Lee and Richard A. Schmidt, "PaR (Plan-act-Review) Golf: Motor Learning Research and Improving Golf Skills," Golf Science Journal, https://www.golfsciencejournal.org/article/5013-par-plan-act-review-golf-motor-learning-research-and-improving-golf-skills

Page 27 "opening yourself up to criticism": Atul Gawande, *The Checklist Manifesto: How to Get Things Right* (Henry Holt & Company, LLC)

CHAPTER 4

Page 32 "I won 22 more tournaments (before retiring)": Beach Volleyball Database, www.bvbinfo.com

Page 45 "Astronauts lose bone mass": Will Dunham, "Astronaut study reveals effects of space travel on human bones," Reuters, https://www.reuters.com/lifestyle/science/astronaut-study-reveals-effects-space-travel-human-bones-2022-07-02/

CHAPTER 5

Page 47 "The Marshmallow Test": Ignitermedia, https://www.youtube.com/watch?v=QX_oy9614HQ&t=17s

Page 49 "Really successful people find a way to show up despite feelings of boredom": James Clear, *Atomic Habits* (Avery)

Page 49 "keep at it,": John Mellencamp, "Living Your Best Life," AARP – The Magazine, February 2, 2022.

Page 50 "Arsene Wenger made changes to the team's off-the-field habits,": TNP (The New Paper), https://tnp.straitstimes.com/sports/football/how-wenger-turned-arsenal-mars-bar-lovers-invincibles

Page 50 "Admiral William McRaven – willpower,": YouTube video of McRaven's 2014 commencement speech at the University of Texas, May 19, 2014. https://www.youtube.com/watch?v=pxBQLFLei70

CHAPTER 8

Page 82 "high-power poses,": YouTube video Amy Cuddy TED Talk: "Your body language may shape who you are," Oct. 1, 2012. https://www.youtube.com/watch?v=Ks-_Mh1QhMc

Page 86 "non-verbal communication,": Shawn Achor, *The Happiness Advantage* (Currency)

CHAPTER 9

Page 93 "emotional vs. logical reactions," Sarah Ewing, "Like thousands of Britons, Olympic hero Chris Hoy was plagued by panic attacks. Then he found an unlikely cure …," Daily Mail, December 23, 2008. https://www.dailymail.co.uk/health/article-1100491/Like-thousands-Britons-Olympic-hero-Chris-Hoy-plagued-panic-attacks-Then-unlikely-cure-.html

Page 95 "accepting your thoughts objectively": Novak Djokovic, *Serve to Win* (Zinc Ink – Ballantine Books)

Page 95 "start with tiny steps": James Clear, *Atomic Habits* (Avery)

CHAPTER 10

Page 107 "dialogue between father and son after the son spills nails": Dr. Haim G. Ginott, *Between Parent and Teenager* (Macmillan)

CHAPTER 11

Page 114 "The Stockdale Paradox": Jim Collins, *Good to Great* (HarperCollins Publishers)

Page 114 "balanced-positive approach": Daniel Coyle, "How to Prepare for a Big Moment," Daniel Coyle Blog. https://danielcoyle.com/blog/page/7/

Page 115 "project premortem": Gary Klein, "Performing a Project Premortem," Harvard Business Review, September, 2007.

CHAPTER 12

Page 140 "using checklists to reduce errors": Atul Gawande, *The Checklist Manifesto: How to Get Things Right* (Henry Holt & Company, LLC)

Page 140 "errors of ignorance, errors of ineptitude": Malcolm Gladwell, "Malcolm Gladwell's review of 'The Checklist Manifesto.'" http://atulgawande.com/book/the-checklist-manifesto/

Page 147 "doing a small number of important things with excellence": Beth Launiere and Leo Hopf, *Stop Competing and Start Winning – The Business of Coaching* (Mastery Publishing, USA)

Page 148 "effective delegation": L. David Marquet, *Turn the Ship Around* (Portfolio/Penguin)

CHAPTER 13

Page 159 "learning by doing": Frank Wilczek, "The Power of Learning by Doing," The Wall Street Journal, January 18, 2017. https://www.wsj.com/articles/the-power-of-learning-by-doing-1484772179

Page 161 "stress triggers a biological response that enhances the ability to learn and grow": Kelly McGonigal, "Embracing Stress is More Important than Reducing Stress," Stanford News, May 7, 2015

INDEX

10,000 hours, 19, 178

Achor, Shawn, 86, 179
Akinradewo, Foluke, 105, 129
Alexander, F. Matthias, 170
amygdala, 90-91
Andretti, Mario, 167
Angelou, Maya, 168
Antunes, Talita, 9, 128
Arsenal, 49, 50
"Atomic Habits," 49, 95, 179, 180

Ball, Lloy, 108-109
Banwarth, Kayla, 125
Bartsch-Hackley, Michelle, 137
Beal, Doug, 124
Bednarczuk, Agatha, 9, 128
Belichick, Bill, 17, 166

Bergmann, Henry, 156
Berzins, Aldis, 20, 65
big rocks, 73, 74, 76, 152
Blanton, Dain, 31, 70
Boskovic, Tijana, 76
Brady, Tom, 7, 17
Brault, Robert, 169
Brigham and Women's Hospital, 140
Brown, Brené, 167
Brubaker, John, 168
Bryant, Kobe, 99-101
Buck, Craig, 12, 34, 123
buddy system, 24
Buffett, Warren, 147

"Cast Away," 93
Ceman, Canyon, 30, 70
checklists, 63, 66, 139, 140-141, 145, 181
Churchill, Winston, 171
Clarke, Arthur C., 168
Clear, James, 49, 95, 169, 170, 177, 179, 180
Cline, Denny, 53
Colberg, Gary, 12
Collins, James C., 113,180
Coyle, Daniel, 114-115, 180
Cuddy, Amy, 82, 179

Dalhausser, Phil, 107-108
debriefing, 27, 60-61, 63
delegating, 146-147
delayed gratification, 47
Dietzen, Christa, 55
DiMaggio, Joe, 6, 177

Djokovic, Novak, 94-95, 96, 180
Doble, Brent, 32
Drews, Annie, 78, 103, 130
drills, 18, 44, 71, 73
Dunphy, Marv, 12, 28, 41, 69, 122
Durant, Kevin, 81-82
Dvorak, Dusty, 34, 122
Dweck, Carol, 170

Egonu, Paola, 130-131
Ehrman, Peter, 162
English Premier League, 49
Enquist, Sue, 135
Epictetus, 169
Epstein, Joseph, 167
Ericsson, Anders, 19-20, 178

Federer, Roger, 94-95
FIVB World Cup, 121
Fonoimoana, Eric, 31
Franca, Larissa, 9, 128
Frankl, Viktor, 127
Frohoff, Brent, 161

Gaffigan, Jim, 51
Gardner, Gabe, 109
Gawande, Atul, 27, 140, 178, 181
Gervais, Mike, 22, 126
Ginott, Haim G., 107, 180
Gladwell, Malcolm, 19, 140, 178, 181
goals, 9, 14, 33, 45, 55, 61, 76, 111, 152
Godin, Seth, 91
"Good to Great," 114, 180

greatness
    absolute, 9, 10
    relative, 9, 10

Halberstam, David, 17, 177
Hancock, Micha, 130, 132, 136
Hanks, Tom, 93
Hansen, Kevin, 109
Hein, Piet, 160
Hill, Kim, 40-41, 62, 86
Hoff, Tom, 109
Holdren, Dax, 31
Hopf, Leo, 146, 181
Hoy, Chris, 89-90, 180
hypothalamus, 91

Il Messaggero Ravenna, 11
intrinsic motivation, 15

James, LeBron, 8
Jansrud, Kjetil, 168
Johnson, Adam, 29-33
Jordan, Michael, 174

Kiraly, Janna, 2, 31, 41, 42
Kiraly, Kati, 56
Kiraly, Kory, 42-43
Kiraly, Kristi, 56
Kiraly, Kristian, 41-43
Kiraly, Las, 126
Kiraly, Toni, 126
Klein, Gary, 115, 181
Krzyzewski, Mike, 81

Lambert, Mike, 32
Lang, Ron, 156
Larson, Jordan, 21, 83, 131
leadership council (LC), 150-151
Lee, Timothy D., 25
Lippmann, Walter, 168
little rocks, 73-74
lizard brain, 91-98, 117
Loiola, Jose, 30-31
Launiere, Beth, 146-147, 181

"Man's Search for Meaning," 127
Manhattan Beach Open, 156, 158
Marlowe, Chris, 38, 123-124
Marquet, David, 148-149, 181
Mars chocolate bars, 50
Marsalis, Wynton, 169
May-Treanor, Misty, 9, 128
McCutcheon, Hugh, 125
McGonigal, Kelly, 161, 182
McGown, Carl, 73
McRaven, William H., 50-52, 179
Mellencamp, John, 49
Menges, Jim, 158
Mentos, 139-140, 142, 151
meritocracy, 17
Miyashiro, Tama, 150
multitasking, 22

Nadal, Rafael, 94-95
Neville, Bill, 11, 13
New England Patriots, 7-8, 17-18, 166
NORCECA zone Continental Championships, 121

Olajuwon, Hakeem, 8
Olmstead, Rick, 13, 52-53
Olympics
    Atlanta, 29-30, 108
    Beijing, 39, 81, 90, 93, 107, 128
    London, 81, 90, 99, 104, 124, 128
    Los Angeles, 34, 36, 121
    Rio de Janeiro, 9, 116, 127
    Seoul, 69-70
    Sydney, 9, 31, 109
    Tokyo, 9, 76-78, 106, 115, 117, 118, 129-132, 134-136,
"Outliers: The Story of Success," 19, 178

"Peak: Secrets from the New Science of Expertise," 19, 178
Piccard, Bertrand, 170
Pickford, Mary, 169
plan-act-review, 25-27, 178
polls (anonymous), 14
poses
    high-power, 82-83, 179
    low-power, 82-83, 179
Poulter, Jordyn, 66, 130-132, 134-135
Powers, Pat, 34, 37, 123, 133
practice
    deliberate, 20, 177, 178
    purposeful, 20, 24, 178
premortem, 115-117, 181
Priddy, Reid, 93

Ragan, Trevor, 91
Rettke, Dana, 151
Riggs, Lou, 38

risk register, 117-121
Robinson, Kelsey, 137
Rogers, Todd, 31, 107-108
Rooney, Sean, 109
Roosevelt, Theodore, 166
Ross, April, 9, 127
Rundle, Larry, 155-156

Saunders, Dave, 122-123
Schmidt, Richard A., 25
Silver, Adam, 99
Slabe, Luka, 45
Smith, David, 106
Smith, Sinjin, 20, 162
Santa Barbara High School, 13, 42, 52
SEAL training, 50-52, 114, 162
Seixas De Freitas, Barbara, 9, 128
Sports Illustrated, 155
St. Margaret's Episcopal School, 41-45
Starr, Ringo, 159-160
static serving, 72
Steffes, Kent, 29, 70
Stitz, Jimmy, 163
Stockdale, James, 113-114, 180
"Stop Competing and Start Winning: The Business of Coaching," 146-147, 181
Stork, Jeff, 122-123
stress management, 82-83, 93, 117, 141, 145, 160-161, 182
surveys (anonymous), 14

Teller, 167
"The Checklist Manifesto," 27, 140, 178, 181
"The Happiness Advantage," 86, 179

The Marshmallow Test, 47-48, 179
The Stockdale Paradox, 114, 180
Thompson, Courtney, 104-106
Thompson, Jordan, 130-131, 134, 136-137
Timmons, Steve, 12, 34, 123, 133
Ting, Zhu, 76
Touzinsky, Scott, 109
Trentor, Alexandra, 168
"Turn the Ship Around," 148, 181
tutoring sessions, 15
Tyson, Mike, 169

USS Santa Fe, 148-149

Von Hagen, Ron, 84, 156

Waitzkin, Joshua, 170
Waldie, Marc, 35,

Walsh Jennings, Kerri, 9, 127-129
Washington, Haleigh, 83-84
Wenger, Arsène, 50, 179
whiteboard, 21, 74, 144-146, 152-154
Wilczek, Frank, 159-160, 166, 181
willpower, 47-50, 52-57
Wong-Orantes, Justine, 21, 131, 136, 151
Wooden, John, 60, 86, 168
World Championship, 13, 34, 36, 70, 124-125, 126
World Cup, 12, 36, 70, 121, 123

ABOUT THE AUTHORS

Karch Kiraly is the head coach of the U.S. women's national volleyball team and one of the greatest players in the sport's history. Under his guidance, the USA women have reached two milestones, winning the first Olympic gold medal in team history (Tokyo, 2021) and the program's first World Championship (Italy, 2014). During  his playing career, Kiraly won three NCAA championships at UCLA and was a key player on the U.S. men's national team that dominated the world in the 1980s, winning consecutive gold medals at the 1984 and '88 OIympics. The Federation of International Volleyball (FIVB) honored him as the world's top player in 1986 and 1988 and has since named him the greatest volleyball player of the 20th Century. In 1996, Kiraly won his third Olympic gold medal in the beach discipline of the game at the Atlanta Games alongside Kent Steffes. In a beach career spanning 25 years, he set an American record with 148 beach tournament titles. He lives with his wife, Janna, in San Clemente, California.

Don Patterson is the senior content manager for The Art of Coaching Volleyball. He was the executive editor of *Volleyball* magazine from 1991-2002. He has also been the editor of *Volleyball USA* and *DiG* magazines and an editor at cbssports.com. He lives in Carlsbad, California, with his wife, Kendal.